# CRUISING GUIDE
# TO INNS AND TAVERNS

## NORFOLK  BROADS

by

## ROSE LEWIS

GW00601597

# COPYRIGHT 1995, ROSE LEWIS

First Published:    March 1990
Second Edition:    June 1991
Third Edition:    November 1992
Reprint:    March 1994
This Edition:    June 1995

British Library Cataloguing in Publication Data
Lewis, Rose

Cruising Guide to Inns and Taverns. Norfolk Broads.
A catalogue record for this book is available from the British Library.

ISBN: 0 9515467 5 9

PUBS WHICH ARE MORE THAN HALF A MILE FROM THE RIVER ARE NOT INCLUDED.

ALL CRUISING TIMES AND DISTANCES ARE APPROXIMATE.

SUMMER TRADING TIMES ARE GENERALLY FROM WHITSUN TO MID SEPTEMBER.

BECAUSE OF THE NEW LAWS REGARDING FACILITIES FOR CHILDREN IT IS BEST TO TELEPHONE AHEAD WHERE THE DESCRIPTION STATES "CHILDREN ARE WELCOME".

**FRONT COVER:**    Approaching Wroxham Bridge from Coltishall

**BACK COVER:**    Map of the Norfolk Broads

PUBLISHED BY:
Rosec Publications
135 Church Road
Shoeburyness
Essex SS3 9EZ

PRINTED IN GREAT BRITAIN BY:
Modern Graphic Arts Ltd
52-54 Milton Road
Westcliff on Sea
Essex SSO 7JX

# INDEX

**THIS EDITION IS IN MEMORY OF "JACK" OF THE DUKES HEAD, SOMERLEYTON**

---

**MY THANKS TO:**

JANE AND DAVID GUILDFORD FOR THEIR LAST MINUTE HELP WITH LITERARY LEADS.

VARIOUS PROPRIETORS FOR NOT CALLING TIME ON MY TENDENCY TO BE TROUBLESOME.

HOSEASONS AND HORIZON CRAFT FOR THEIR HELP WITH BOAT HIRE.

**MY LOVE TO:**

MY MOTHER, FOR LAUGHTER AND LINE DRAWINGS.

CHRIS, MY HUSBAND, FOR BEING MAGNANIMOUS OVER MISSED MEALS, TAKING PHOTOGRAPHS AND DRAWING MAPS WHILST MAKING MOLEHILLS OUT OF ALL MY MOUNTAINS AND MANAGING TO MANOEUVRE AND MOOR WHILST NOT MENTIONING MY NAVIGATIONAL MISHAPS

R. L.

---

THE AUTHOR AND PUBLISHERS OF THIS BOOK WELCOME ANY COMMENTS FROM THEIR READERS, GOOD OR BAD. PLEASE WRITE TO:

ROSEC PUBLICATIONS
135 CHURCH ROAD
SHOEBURYNESS
ESSEX SS3 9EZ

# INTRODUCTION

Unlike the roadways of Britain there are no signposts on the waterways of the Norfolk Broads, one cannot travel after dark and it can take a fair while to "pull up at a pub".

For those who enjoy a decent drink and a good meal in congenial surroundings this river by river guide allows you to see at a glance the choices of venue open to you, the moorings available and the distances and times between your destination, wherever you may find yourself.

After several attempts to navigate my way via various maps and advertisements in an endeavour to discover the welcoming hostelry that must surely be round the next bend in the river, I wrote this Guide - if only to help others "in the same boat".

There are many changes in this Edition. For the sake of new holiday makers, and because of numerous letters received, I have decided to include more detail for the routes and rivers which I trust everyone will benefit from. Over the years some of the pubs have closed down or been converted. I hope that the new pubs in this book (as well as those that remain) will bring you many happy hours and I can only reiterate what I have always said in all my books:

"Have a marvellous holiday and good luck with steering your bedroom to the bar"!

**Rose Lewis**
**May 1995**

# THE RIVER ANT - DISTANCES AND TIMINGS

## MOUTH OF THE ANT TO WAYFORD BRIDGE AND STALHAM

MOUTH OF ANT TO LUDHAM BRIDGE = 1 MILE - 20 MINUTES
LUDHAM BRIDGE TO NEATISHEAD (BARTON ANGLER, WHITE HORSE) = 5 MILES - 1 HOUR
NEATISHEAD TO WAYFORD BRIDGE (WOODFARM INN) = 3 MILES - 45 MINUTES
WAYFORD BRIDGE TO STALHAM = 3 MILES - 45 MINUTES
NEATISHEAD TO STALHAM (SWAN INN, KINGFISHER HOTEL) = 3 MILES - 45 MINUTES

## STALHAM AND WAYFORD BRIDGE TO MOUTH OF THE ANT

STALHAM (SWAN INN, KINGFISHER HOTEL) TO NEATISHEAD = 3 MILES - 45 MINUTES
STALHAM TO WAYFORD BRIDGE = 3 MILES - 45 MINUTES
WAYFORD BRIDGE (WOODFARM INN) TO NEATISHEAD = 3 MILES - 45 MINUTES
NEATISHEAD (BARTON ANGLER, WHITE HORSE) TO LUDHAM BRIDGE = 5 MILES - 1 HOUR
LUDHAM BRIDGE TO MOUTH OF ANT = 1 MILE - 20 MINUTES

# THE RIVER ANT

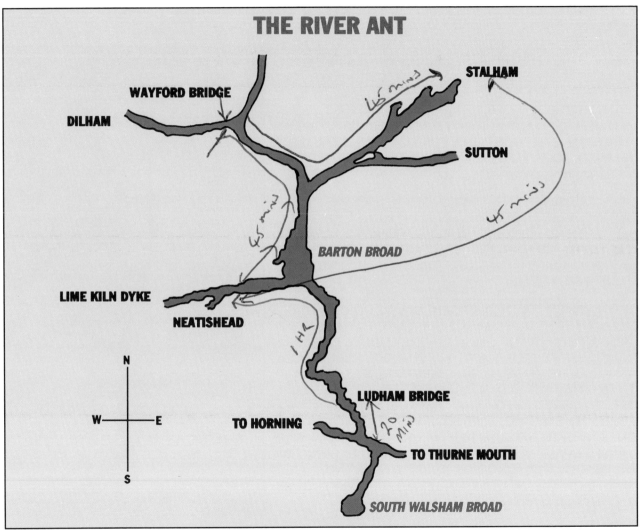

STALHAM

WAYFORD BRIDGE

DILHAM

SUTTON

45 mins

45 mins

45 mins

BARTON BROAD

LIME KILN DYKE

NEATISHEAD

1 HR

N

W——E

S

LUDHAM BRIDGE

TO HORNING

20 Min

TO THURNE MOUTH

SOUTH WALSHAM BROAD

# THE RIVER ANT

THIS RIVER IS EXTREMELY POPULAR DURING THE FISHING SEASON. THE MOUTH OF THE RIVER ANT LIES BETWEEN, AND ON THE OPPOSITE SIDE TO, RANWORTH BROAD AND SOUTH WALSHAM BROAD ON THE BURE. ONCE UNDER LUDHAM BRIDGE YOU WILL FIND GOOD MOORINGS TO YOUR RIGHT AND LEFT, AND LUDHAM BRIDGE SERVICES, ON THE RIGHT BANK, IS A GOOD PLACE FOR VICTUALS. "THE DOG" PUBLIC HOUSE (11.30 TO 3 AND 6.30 TO 11) IS FURTHER DOWN ON THE SAME ROAD.

AS YOU CRUISE FURTHER UPSTREAM YOU WILL PASS HOW HILL NATURE RESERVE ON YOUR RIGHT. HERE YOU WILL ALSO FIND TOAD HOLE COTTAGE WHERE YOU CAN BUY TICKETS FOR A TRIP ON THE "ELECTRIC EEL", A NOISELESS BOAT FROM WHICH YOU CAN SEE THE NUMEROUS WILDLIFE ON THE WATER TRAIL.

WHEN CROSSING BARTON BROAD, AS YOU GO UPSTREAM, KEEP ALL RED STAKES TO YOUR LEFT, AND TO YOUR RIGHT WHEN RETURNING. YOU CAN PASS EITHER SIDE OF PLEASURE HILL ISLAND WHICH IS SOON TO BE ENTIRELY REBUILT AS A LANDMARK. TO CRUISE TO NEATISHEAD KEEP TO THE LEFT AS YOU ENTER THE BROAD AND TAKE THE FIRST MAIN LEFT FORK. TO VISIT BARTON TURF BEAR RIGHT ACROSS THE BROAD AND TAKE THE LEFT FORK WHERE INDICATED. TO CONTINUE UP TO WAYFORD BRIDGE (HEIGHT AT HIGH WATER 7') AND DILHAM, KEEP TO THE RIGHT FORK. IF GOING TO STALHAM OR SUTTON BEAR RIGHT WHERE INDICATED FURTHER UPSTREAM AND THEN BEAR LEFT FOR STALHAM OR RIGHT FOR SUTTON.

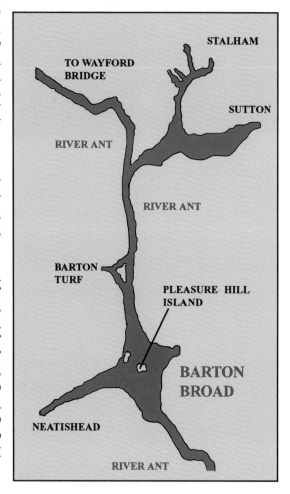

# NEATISHEAD

*LUNCH WED?*

## BARTON ANGLER COUNTRY INN TEL: (01692) 630740

### 5 MILES FROM LUDHAM BRIDGE - 1 HOUR
### 3 MILES TO STALHAM OR SUTTON BROAD - 45 MINUTES
### 3 MILES TO WAYFORD BRIDGE - 45 MINUTES

**MOORINGS:** There are several at "Gays Staithe" - just before steering round to Lime Kiln Dyke. Mostly stern on. No fees. Distance to the hotel is 200 yards.

| | |
|---|---|
| **SUMMER:** | 11.30 to 2.30 and 6.30 to 11 |
| **WINTER:** | 12 to 2.30 and 7 to 11 |
| **SUNDAY:** | 12 to 3 and 7 to 10.30 |
| | |
| **BEERS:** | Greene King, IPA, Abbot and Rayments |
| **LAGERS:** | Kronenberg 1664 |
| **CIDERS:** | Red Rock |
| | |
| **SPECIALITIES:** | Fresh Fish Pie. Steak and Ale Pie. All food is freshly prepared and cooked by the Chef. |
| | |
| **SUNDAY LUNCH:** | Bar menu and full Restaurant service |
| | |
| **BAR MEALS:** | Noon to 2.30 and 7 to 9 (Last Orders 2 pm and 9 pm) |

**DINING FACILITIES:** Room for 36. 7.30 to 11.30 (Last Orders 9 pm). Open every evening. Booking advisable. Typical cost of three course meal for two with wine: £25.

**CARDS:** (Restaurant only): Access, Visa, Amex.

*An old rectory house set in four acres of landscaped gardens. Dogs welcome. Seating enough for 70 people amongst the lovely Azalea and Rhododendron beds. A well furnished A La Carte restaurant is provided along with pleasantly soft background music.*

*Full hotel accommodation is available with two rooms boasting four-poster beds. Bar-B-Q's are held in the summer and rowing boats may be hired from here. Is there a ghost in Bedroom No. 1?*

*Lord Nelson often visited as a boy and learnt to sail on nearby Barton Broad.*

# NEATISHEAD

## THE WHITE HORSE   TEL: (01692) 630828

**5 MILES FROM LUDHAM BRIDGE - 1 HOUR**
**3 MILES TO STALHAM OR SUTTON BROAD - 45 MINUTES**
**3 MILES TO WAYFORD BRIDGE - 45 MINUTES**

**MOORINGS:** Several, side on, in Lime Kiln Dyke. These are free for 24 hours and are 300 yards from the pub. Torches required at night.

| | |
|---|---|
| **SUMMER:** | 11 to 3 and 7 to 11 |
| **WINTER:** | 12 to 2.30 and 7.30 to 11 |
| **SUNDAY:** | 12 to 3 and 7 to 10.30 |

| | |
|---|---|
| **BEERS:** | Flowers, Greene King, IPA, Tolly Original and Guest Beers |
| **LAGERS:** | Stella Artois and Castlemaine XXXX |
| **CIDERS:** | Red Rock |

**SPECIALITIES:**   Duck. Plaice on the bone.

**SUNDAY LUNCH:**   £4.75 per head (1994)

**BAR MEALS:**   12 to 2.30 and 7.30 to 9.30 (Last Orders 2 pm and 9.15 pm)

**DINING FACILITIES:** Seating for 25. 12 to 2.30 and 7.30 to 9.30 (Last Orders 2 pm and 9.15 pm). Typical cost of three course meal for two with wine: £20.

**CARDS:** Cheque with bankers card.

*This 500 year old hostelry of great character holds the Broads Authority Award for High Service. The red brick building supports trellises of roses and passion flowers. Friendly service in homely surroundings.*

*One room is full of Broadlands memorabilia whilst another boasts an agricultural museum. A traditional Norfolk bar leads to the childrens room and dining salon. Folk nights are held once a month. Details on request.*

*Lime Kiln Dyke is an attractive wooded area with a turning basin at its apex.*

# WAYFORD BRIDGE

## WOODFARM INN    TEL: (01692) 582414

**3 MILES FROM NEATISHEAD - 45 MINUTES**
**3 MILES TO STALHAM OR SUTTON BROAD - 45 MINUTES**
**1 MILE TO DILHAM - 20 MINUTES**

**MOORINGS:** Numerous on both banks either side of bridge. A nominal fee is requested after 5.30 if staying overnight on the West bank. Distance to the pub is 100/300 yards dependant on where you moor. Torches useful at night.

| | |
|---|---|
| **SUMMER:** | All day |
| **WINTER:** | All day |
| **SUNDAY:** | 12 to 3 and 7 to 10.30 |
| | |
| **BEERS:** | Eighteen in all |
| **LAGERS:** | Stella Artois, Heineken, Black Label |
| **CIDERS:** | Strongbow |
| | |
| **SPECIALITIES:** | Grills and vegetarian menus. |
| | |
| **SUNDAY LUNCH:** | £3.95 per head (1994) |
| | |
| **BAR MEALS:** | Full Menu available all day. Full English breakfasts. |

**DINING FACILITIES:** Seating for 140. 11.30 to 10 (Last Orders 9.30 pm - Summer and 9 pm - Winter). Typical cost of three course meal for two with wine: £15.

**CARDS:** Diners Club and cheques with bankers card.

*A large, "value for money", Freehouse set in five acres of rural Broadland. The three bars, lounge and Portuguese style restaurant command excellent views of the river.*

*A childrens' room, amusements and satellite TV provide entertainment for all the family. Ask about the Duck Pond, Barn and Stable and the Pightle. "Can you possibly eat it all" breakfasts from £3 are served from 8.30 am - Monday to Saturday, from March to the end of September.*

*During the summer Bar-B-Q's are held in the beer gardens on Fridays, Saturdays and Sundays.*

# STALHAM

## THE KINGFISHER HOTEL    TEL: (01692) 581974

**3 MILES FROM NEATISHEAD - 45 MINUTES**
**3 MILES TO WAYFORD BRIDGE - 45 MINUTES**

**MOORINGS:** Numerous free areas in and around the various boatyards and Stalham Dyke. The pub is at the top of the High Street - approximately 1/4 mile from the moorings.

| | |
|---|---|
| **SUMMER:** | 11 to 2.30 and 6 to 11 |
| **WINTER:** | 11 to 2.30 and 6 to 11 |
| **SUNDAY:** | 12 to 2.30 and 7 to 10.30 |
| **BEERS:** | Adnams, Wherry, Bass, Stones, Guinness and Caffreys |
| **LAGERS:** | Tennants and Carling Black Label |
| **CIDERS:** | Dry Blackthorn |
| **SPECIALITIES:** | Whole pan fried sole coated with almonds. Char grilled fillet steak with wild mushrooms. |
| **SUNDAY LUNCH:** | Main course £4.75 (1994) |
| **BAR MEALS:** | Noon to 2 and 7 to 9 (Last Orders 2 pm and 9 pm) |

**DINING FACILITIES:** Seating for 40. Noon to 2 and 7 to 9 (Last Orders 2 pm and 8.45 pm). Typical cost of three course meal for two with wine: £30.
**CARDS:** Access and Visa.

*Not previously featured in the Guide this Hotel has often been recommended as a good venue.*

*Set in the heart of this small market town the Kingfisher, with its en-suite bedrooms and pleasant decor, is justly known for its extensive menus - specialising in local seafood dishes.*

*There is one bar and no games or music are provided - making this a refreshing change for some. The landscaped gardens are especially attractive. Dogs welcome. Children are allowed in the bar and no-smoking restaurant and there are good facilities for the disabled, with ramp access.*

# STALHAM

## THE SWAN INN    TEL: (01692) 581492

**3 MILES FROM NEATISHEAD - 45 MINUTES**
**3 MILES TO WAYFORD BRIDGE - 45 MINUTES**

**MOORINGS:** Numerous free areas in and around the various boatyards and Stalham Dyke. The pub is on your left - before you reach the Kingfisher Hotel - in the middle of the High Street.

| | |
|---|---|
| **SUMMER:** | 11 to 2.30 and 7 to 11 |
| | All day Friday and Saturday |
| **WINTER:** | As above |
| **SUNDAY:** | 12 to 3 and 7 to 10.30 |
| **BEERS:** | Adnams real ales, Guest Ales, John Smiths Bitter, Whitbread Mild, Murphys and Guinness |
| **LAGERS:** | Stella Artois and Heineken |
| **CIDERS:** | Red Rock |
| **SPECIALITIES:** | Stilton and walnut steak. Home made steak and kidney pie. Garlic Prawns. |
| **SUNDAY LUNCH**: | Main menu available |
| **BAR MEALS:** | Noon to 2 and 7 to 9 (Last Orders 2 pm and 9 pm) |

**DINING FACILITIES:** Seating for 20 and anywhere in pub. Noon to 2 and 7 to 9. Last Orders as for bar meals.
**CARDS:** Cheque with bankers card.

*Stalham Lions, R.A.O.B. and the British Legion meet regularly in this sociable and welcoming pub where the lounge bar is wood panelled with warm red furnishing, soft lighting and background music. A charity book sale in aid of the Stalham Lions and the local R.N.L.I. is held here.*

*The public bar provides a juke box, pool table and dart board whilst in the small dining room an unusual feature is the "pottery" room heater. A comprehensive menu is served in all rooms.*

*There is good access for wheelchairs to all areas.*

# THE RIVER THURNE - DISTANCES AND TIMINGS

## MOUTH OF THE THURNE TO HICKLING AND WEST SOMERTON

MOUTH OF THE THURNE TO THURNE (THE LION) = 1/2 MILE - 15 MINUTES
THURNE TO POTTER HEIGHAM (FALGATE, BROADSHAVEN TAVERN)
                               = 4 MILES - 45 MINUTES
POTTER HEIGHAM TO HICKLING BROAD (PLEASURE BOAT INN) = 4 1/2 MILES - 1 HOUR
POTTER HEIGHAM TO WEST SOMERTON (THE LION) = 4 1/2 MILES - 1 HOUR
POTTER HEIGHAM TO HORSEY MERE = 4 MILES - 1 HOUR

## HICKLING AND WEST SOMERTON TO MOUTH OF THE THURNE

HORSEY MERE TO POTTER HEIGHAM = 4 MILES - 1 HOUR
WEST SOMERTON (THE LION) TO POTTER HEIGHAM = 4 1/2 MILES - 1 HOUR
HICKLING BROAD (PLEASURE BOAT INN) TO POTTER HEIGHAM = 4 1/2 MILES - 1 HOUR
POTTER HEIGHAM (FALGATE, BROADSHAVEN TAVERN) TO THURNE
                               = 4 MILES - 45 MINUTES
THURNE (THE LION) TO MOUTH OF THE THURNE = 1/2 MILE - 15 MINUTES

# THE RIVER THURNE

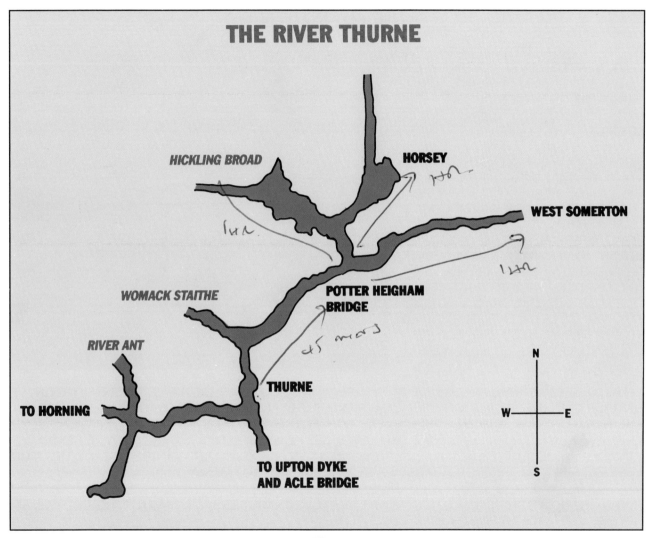

# THE RIVER THURNE

JUST PAST THE MOUTH OF THE THURNE IS ST. BENET'S LEVEL WINDPUMP ON YOUR LEFT AND THURNE DYKE WINDPUMP ON YOUR RIGHT WHICH IS OPEN DURING DAYLIGHT HOURS IN SUMMER.

PASSING WOMACK STAITHE (WHERE YOU CAN WALK FROM MOORINGS TO THE "KINGS HEAD" AT LUDHAM AND WHERE THE NORFOLK WHERRY TRUST IS SITUATED) YOU WILL COME TO POTTER HEIGHAM PASSING MANY LITTLE WATERSIDE CHALETS, SOME WITH EXTREMELY PRETTY FACADES AND GARDENS. IN PARTICULAR LOOK OUT FOR AN UNUSUAL LOOKING COTTAGE ON YOUR LEFT, PURPORTED TO ONCE HAVE BEEN THE TOP OF A HELTER-SKELTER RIDE AT GREAT YARMOUTH!

ON TO POTTER HEIGHAM, FAMOUS FOR ITS BRIDGE (PICTURED ABOVE), LATHAMS STORES AND "CRINGLES RESTAURANT". AT THE BRIDGE YOU MUST WAIT FOR THE PILOT IF YOU WISH TO TRAVEL FURTHER AS THE HEIGHT OF THE BRIDGE IS ONLY 6'9" AT THE CENTRE POINT AT HIGH WATER. ONCE UNDER THE BRIDGE YOU WILL PASS HIGH'S MILL ON YOUR RIGHT. OPPOSITE THIS IS CANDLE DYKE LEADING TO HEIGHAM SOUND AND THEN, VIA A LEFT HAND FORK, TO HICKLING BROAD. IF YOU TAKE THE RIGHT FORK YOU WILL GO THROUGH MEADOW DYKE WHICH LEADS TO HORSEY MERE.

IF YOU ARE GOING DIRECTLY TO WEST SOMERTON KEEP ON PAST THE TURNING TO CANDLE DYKE AND STAY ON THE MAIN RIVER TO SOMERTON STAITHE.

# THURNE ✓

## THE LION  TEL: (01692) 670796

### 1/2 MILE FROM THURNE MOUTH - 15 MINUTES
### 4 MILES TO POTTER HEIGHAM - 45 MINUTES

**MOORINGS:** Approximately 30 side on. There is no charge for mooring on the left hand bank but a small fee is requested for those on the right. The distance to the pub is 100/300 yards. Torches may be useful at night.

| | |
|---|---|
| **SUMMER:** | 11 to 3 and 6 to 11 |
| **WINTER:** | 11 to 2 and 7 to 11 |
| **SUNDAY:** | 12 to 3 and 7 to 10.30 |
| | |
| **BEERS:** | Six Traditional Ales, two Stouts and one Keg beer. |
| **LAGERS:** | Heineken, Stella Artois and Heineken Export |
| **CIDERS:** | Scrumpy Jack |
| | |
| **SPECIALITIES:** | Twenty four home made dishes plus a very large range of others. |
| | |
| **SUNDAY LUNCH:** | Roasts and main menu available. |
| | |
| **BAR MEALS:** | Noon to 2 and Opening to 9.30 (Last Orders 2 pm and 9.30 pm) |

**DINING FACILITIES:** Seating for 135 inside and 150 outside. Times as above. Typical cost of three course meal for two with wine: £20.
**CARDS:** Visa, Access, Amex, Switch, JCB and Mastercard.

*Sometimes it is difficult to know how best to describe a pub but with this one it is definitely the "Atmosphere". A purpose built restaurant/function room was completed in 1994.*

*An old Victorian House with traditional decor and open fires, pool table, amusements and a family room. Soft background music. Dogs are allowed and a mini Zoo and Crazy Golf are on offer. Full facilities for the disabled are available.*

*A windmill and a restored windpump stand near the entrance to the dyke.*

# POTTER HEIGHAM

## BROADSHAVEN TAVERN  TEL: (01692) 670329

### 4 MILES FROM THURNE - 45 MINUTES
### 4 1/2 MILES TO HICKLING AND WEST SOMERTON - 1 HOUR

**MOORINGS:** Both alongside the bank and in the basin. There is no charge and the distance to the tavern is 100 to 300 yards, to the left of the Bridge, on the opposite side of the road.

| | |
|---|---|
| **SUMMER:** | All day |
| **WINTER:** | 11 to 2.30 and 6.30 to 11 |
| **SUNDAY:** | 12 to 3 and 7 to 10.30 |
| | |
| **BEERS:** | Tetley, Poachers, Worthington Best, IPA, Guinness and Murphys |
| **LAGERS:** | Carlsberg, Stella and Carling |
| **CIDERS:** | Dry Blackthorn |
| | |
| **SPECIALITIES:** | Smoked salmon.  Carpet bagger. Childrens menu. |
| | |
| **SUNDAY LUNCH:** | Main course - £3.90 (1994) |
| | |
| **BAR MEALS:** | Noon to 2 and 6 to 10 (Last Orders 2 pm and 9.30 pm) |

**DINING FACILITIES:** Seating for 100. Times as for bar meals. Typical cost of three course meal for two with wine: £20.
**CARDS:** Cheque with bankers card.

*Since the Bridge Inn burnt down in the Spring of 1992 this is now the only place to eat, drink and watch the fun whilst sitting near the famous Bridge.*

*The Admirals Bar and Sandy's Bar are both pleasantly decorated and the restaurant is spacious and overlooks the river. Disco nights are frequently held.*

*A fruit machine, darts and two pool tables are provided and there is a separate room for those with families.*

*You are welcome to bring your dog here and there are good facilities for the disabled.*

# POTTER HEIGHAM

## THE FALGATE INN    TEL: (01692) 670003

**4 MILES FROM THURNE - 45 MINUTES**
**4 1/2 MILES TO HICKLING AND WEST SOMERTON - 1 HOUR**

**MOORINGS:** Both alongside the bank and in the basin. There is no charge and the distance to the pub is 800 yards. Turn left at the Bridge and go past a small estate. Torches useful at night.

| | |
|---|---|
| **SUMMER:** | 11 to 3 and 6 to 11 |
| **WINTER:** | 11 to 3 and 6 to 11 |
| **SUNDAY:** | 12 to 3 and 7 to 10.30 |

| | |
|---|---|
| **BEERS:** | Four real ales plus keg beers |
| **LAGERS:** | Stella Artois and Carlsberg |
| **CIDERS:** | Dry Blackthorn |

**SPECIALITIES:** Selection of Home cooked pies. Vegetarian and childrens menu.

**SUNDAY LUNCH:** £3.95 per head (1994). Very popular so it may be wise to book ahead

**BAR MEALS:** Noon to 2.30 and 7 to 10 (Last Orders 2 pm and 9.30 pm).

**DINING FACILITIES:** Seating for 26. 7 to 11 (Last Orders 9.30 pm). Typical cost of three course meal for two with wine: £25.
**CARDS:** Visa and Access

*A large old village Inn which was once a Toll House. In the lounge bar the focal point is the fine Tudor fireplace surrounded by horse brasses.*

*The A La Carte restaurant is intimate and tastefully decorated and it would be a shame to miss out on the Falgate's own excellent wine.*

*Background music, a family room, dartboard and beer garden are provided. Dogs allowed in bar or garden only. Bed and full English breakfast.*

*On 27th February 1993 the thatched roof of the pub caught fire and the Falgate only reopened in November of that year.*

# HICKLING BROAD

11²?

## PLEASURE BOAT INN     TEL: (01692) 598211

**4 1/2 MILES FROM POTTER HEIGHAM - 1 HOUR
2 MILES TO WEST SOMERTON - 30 MINUTES**

**MOORINGS:**  These are plentiful and side on.  There is no charge and the pub is 100/300 yards away.

| | |
|---|---|
| **SUMMER:** | All day |
| **WINTER:** | 11 to 2.30 and 6.30 to 11 |
| **SUNDAY:** | 12 to 3 and 7 to 10.30 |
| | |
| **BEERS:** | Simonds, Websters, Guinness and Guest Beers |
| **LAGERS:** | Fosters and Kronenbourg |
| **CIDERS:** | Strongbow and Woodpecker |
| | |
| **SPECIALITIES:** | Selection of seafood and a range of vegetarian and home cooked food. |
| | |
| **SUNDAY LUNCH:** | Main menu available |
| | |
| **BAR MEALS:** | Noon to 2.30 and 7 to 9  (Last Orders 2 pm and 9 pm) |

**DINING FACILITIES:**  Seating for 42.  Noon to 2.30 and 7 to 9.30 (Last Orders 2.15 pm  and 9.15 pm). Typical cost of three course meal for two with wine:  £20.
**CARDS:**  Access and Visa.

*A popular pub with large and airy rooms, pool table, juke box and a play garden with wildfowl. Dogs welcome.*

*Holidaymakers seem to enjoy themselves here as there is a free and easy atmosphere.  A good A La Carte/Speciality menu is now available.*

*Hickling Broad is the largest lake in Broadlands and was designated as a National Nature Reserve in 1945.*

*A water trail begins near the pub where it is possible to travel on a replica of a traditional reed-carrying boat known as a "lighter".*

# WEST SOMERTON

## THE LION   TEL: (01493) 393289

**4 1/2 MILES FROM POTTER HEIGHAM - 1 HOUR
2 MILES TO HICKLING BROAD - 30 MINUTES**

**MOORINGS:** There is room for approximately 40 side on along the dyke, bearing right. There is no charge and the distance to the pub is 400 yards going up the hill and either across the field or round this using the road. Torches required at night.

| | |
|---|---|
| **SUMMER:** | 11 to 3.30 and 6 to 11 |
| **WINTER:** | 11 to 3.30 and 6 to 11 |
| **SUNDAY:** | 12 to 3 and 7 to 10.30 |
| | |
| **BEERS:** | Abbot, Greene King, IPA, McEwans Export, Whitbread Best, Guinness and selected Guest Traditional Ales. |
| **LAGERS:** | Heineken and Stella Artois |
| **CIDERS:** | Strongbow |
| | |
| **SPECIALITIES:** | Roast Duckling. T-Bone Steaks. King Prawns in Garlic Butter. |
| | |
| **SUNDAY LUNCH:** | Main menu available |
| | |
| **BAR MEALS:** | 11 to 3 and 6 to 10 (Last Orders 2.45 pm and 9.45 pm) |

**DINING FACILITIES:** Seating for 40. 11 to 3 and 6 to 10 (Last Orders 2.45 pm and 9.45 pm). Typical cost of two course meal for two with wine: £20.
**CARDS:** Cheque with bankers card.

*This Freehouse enjoys agreeable hospitality and comfort. It is tastefully decorated and inglenook seating makes for privacy if you feel so inclined.*

*Willing and cheerful staff give lively service in the lounge and saloon bars and the local residents are happy to mingle and chat with visiting river travellers.*

*A pool table is in use in the Winter months and a dartboard is available all year round. Dogs are welcome and there is also a childrens room.*

# THE RIVER BURE - DISTANCES AND TIMINGS

## COLTISHALL TO GREAT YARMOUTH

COLTISHALL (RED LION, KINGS HEAD, RISING SUN) TO WROXHAM (THE CASTLE)
= 4 MILES - 45 MINUTES
WROXHAM TO WROXHAM BRIDGE (KINGS HEAD HOTEL) = 1 MILE - 10 MINUTES
WROXHAM BRIDGE TO HORNING (THE SWAN, THE FERRY) = 5 MILES - 1 HOUR
HORNING TO RANWORTH (THE MALTSTERS) = 3 MILES - 30 MINUTES
RANWORTH TO THURNE MOUTH = 3 MILES - 30 MINUTES
(ANT MOUTH TO THURNE MOUTH = 1 MILE - 10 MINUTES)
THURNE MOUTH TO UPTON DYKE (WHITE HORSE) = 2 MILES - 20 MINUTES
UPTON DYKE TO ACLE BRIDGE (THE BRIDGE) = 1 MILE - 10 MINUTES
ACLE BRIDGE TO STOKESBY (THE FERRY INN) = 2 MILES - 20 MINUTES
STOKESBY TO TUNSTALL (THE STRACEY ARMS) = 2 MILES - 20 MINUTES
TUNSTALL TO GREAT YARMOUTH (SUSPENSION BRIDGE TAVERN) = 8 MILES - 1 1/2 HOURS

## GREAT YARMOUTH TO COLTISHALL

GREAT YARMOUTH (SUSPENSION BRIDGE TAVERN) TO TUNSTALL = 8 MILES - 1 1/2 HOURS
TUNSTALL (STRACEY ARMS) TO STOKESBY = 2 MILES - 20 MINUTES
STOKESBY (THE FERRY INN) TO ACLE BRIDGE = 2 MILES - 20 MINUTES
ACLE BRIDGE (THE BRIDGE) TO UPTON DYKE = 1 MILE - 10 MINUTES
UPTON DYKE (THE WHITE HORSE) TO THURNE MOUTH = 2 MILES - 20 MINUTES
(THURNE MOUTH TO ANT MOUTH = 1 MILE - 10 MINUTES)
THURNE MOUTH TO RANWORTH = 3 MILES - 30 MINUTES
RANWORTH (THE MALTSTERS) TO HORNING = 3 MILES - 30 MINUTES
HORNING (THE FERRY, THE SWAN) TO WROXHAM BRIDGE = 5 MILES - 1 HOUR
WROXHAM BRIDGE (KINGS HEAD HOTEL) TO WROXHAM = 1 MILE - 10 MINUTES
WROXHAM (CASTLE) TO COLTISHALL (RED LION, KINGS HEAD, RISING SUN)
= 4 MILES - 45 MINUTES

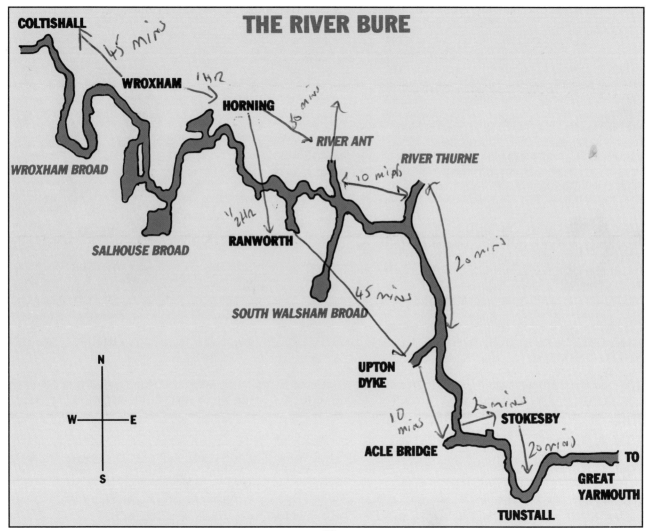

# THE RIVER BURE

COLTISHALL

45 mins

WROXHAM

1 HR

HORNING

30 mins

RIVER ANT

RIVER THURNE

WROXHAM BROAD

10 mins

½ HR

20 mins

SALHOUSE BROAD

RANWORTH

45 mins

SOUTH WALSHAM BROAD

UPTON DYKE

N

W — E

S

10 mins

20 mins

STOKESBY

20 mins

ACLE BRIDGE

TO GREAT YARMOUTH

TUNSTALL

# THE RIVER BURE

COLTISHALL IS THE HEAD OF NAVIGATION ON THIS RIVER WHICH RUNS FOR OVER 30 MILES DOWN TO GREAT YARMOUTH. ONE OF THE PRETTIEST STRETCHES ON THE BROADS IS FROM COLTISHALL TO WROXHAM.

WROXHAM BRIDGE (BUILT IN 1614) MUST ONLY BE NAVIGATED AT LOW TIDES. (HEIGHT 7'3" AT HIGH WATER). WROXHAM IS ONE OF THE BEST PLACES TO SHOP AND FROM HERE YOU CAN VISIT WROXHAM BARNS OR TAKE A 9 MILE TRIP ON THE BURE VALLEY RAILWAY TO AYLSHAM.

BEFORE REACHING HORNING YOU PASS WROXHAM BROAD, HOVETON GREAT BROAD NATURE TRAIL, SALHOUSE BROAD AND SALHOUSE VILLAGE WHERE THERE IS AN EQUESTRIAN CENTRE. HORNING STRETCHES FOR QUITE A WAY AND YOU MAY SEE THE "SOUTHERN COMFORT" PADDLE STEAMER PLYING BACK AND FORTH BETWEEN HERE AND RANWORTH DYKE ALMOST OPPOSITE THE ANT MOUTH. THE ENTRANCE TO RANWORTH IS HERE, THROUGH MALTHOUSE BROAD.

THE DISTANCE BETWEEN THE ANT MOUTH AND THE THURNE MOUTH IS ONE MILE. TWO MILES FURTHER ON IS THE ENTRANCE TO UPTON DYKE ON YOUR RIGHT. ACLE BRIDGE COMES NEXT AND THEN STOKESBY WITH ITS CANDLEMAKING AND MODEL CENTRE.

ON NOW TO TUNSTALL AND THE "STRACEY ARMS" ON YOUR RIGHT. THIS IS THE LAST PLACE TO MOOR BEFORE THE STRETCH TO GREAT YARMOUTH (MOORINGS PICTURED ABOVE) WHERE NUMEROUS ATTRACTIONS MAY KEEP YOU ENTERTAINED FOR A WHILE. HORSE DRAWN CARRIAGES, TREASURE WORLD, CRAZY GOLF, THE HOUSE OF WAX, REGENT BOWL (TEN PIN BOWLING), WELLINGTON AND BRITANNIA PIERS, MARINA LEISURE CENTRE, PLEASURE BEACH FAIRGROUND, RIPLEY'S ODDITORIUM, THE SEA LIFE CENTRE, BUTTERFLY FARM AND MERRIVALE MODEL VILLAGE ARE ALL NEARBY. THERE ARE ALSO MANY EXCELLENT RESTAURANTS AND BEACHES.

## COLTISHALL

### THE RISING SUN     TEL: (01603) 737440

**4 MILES TO WROXHAM - 45 MINUTES**

**MOORINGS:** Approximately 35 side on. There is no fee for the first 24 hours and the pub is 50 to 500 yards away.

| | |
|---|---|
| **SUMMER:** | All day (June to September) |
| **WINTER:** | 11 to 3 and 6 to 11 |
| **SUNDAY:** | 12 to 3 and 7 to 10.30 |

| | |
|---|---|
| **BEERS:** | Theakstons Best, Websters Yorkshire, John Smiths and Directors |
| **LAGERS:** | Holsten, Fosters and Carlsberg |
| **CIDERS:** | Strongbow and Woodpecker |

**SPECIALITIES:**     Steak and Kidney pie, Sirloin Steak, Gammon Steak.

**SUNDAY LUNCH:**     Main Course - £4.75.  Sweets - £1.85

**BAR MEALS:**     Noon to 2.30  and 7 to 9.30  (Last Orders 2 pm and 9.30 pm.  10 pm on Saturdays)

**DINING FACILITIES:**  Seating for 60.  Meal times as above. Typical cost of  three course meal for two with wine: £20.
**CARDS:**  Visa, Access, Diners and Amex.

*Situated on an old public staithe once used by traditional Norfolk Wherries this is a well known hostelry - originally  a grain store and maltings.*

*Smartened up externally with white paint and hanging baskets the pub still retains its character. A rambling interior is dotted with Chesterfields, lounge chairs and interesting photographs of the old days in the two bars.  Music is supplied by background tapes and pool is available.  Dogs allowed.*

*An extremely large patio lies adjacent to a play area. Children are also welcome in the Granary restaurant which overlooks the river and is a no-smoking area. A separate dining room is provided as are excellent facilities for the disabled.*

# COLTISHALL

## THE KINGS HEAD          TEL: (01603) 737426

### 4 MILES TO WROXHAM - 45 MINUTES

**MOORINGS:** These are plentiful and side on. There is no charge for the first 24 hours and you will find the Kings Head tucked just behind the Rising Sun, on your left as you approach the road.

| | |
|---|---|
| **SUMMER:** | All day (May to mid September) |
| **WINTER:** | 11 to 3 and 7 to 11 |
| **SUNDAY:** | 12 to 3 and 7 to 10.30 |

| | |
|---|---|
| **BEERS:** | Ruddles County, Yardarm, Adnams, Websters, Guinness, Directors, Beamish and Guest Beers |
| **LAGERS:** | Holsten Export, Carlsberg and Fosters |
| **CIDERS:** | Strongbow and Redrock |

| | |
|---|---|
| **SPECIALITIES:** | Pacific Prawns in Garlic Butter. Medallions of Beef Fillet. |

| | |
|---|---|
| **SUNDAY LUNCH:** | £4.95 per head (1994) |

| | |
|---|---|
| **BAR MEALS:** | Noon to 2 and 7 to 9.30 (Last Orders 1.45 pm and 9.30 pm) |

**DINING FACILITIES:** Seating for 50. Times as above. Typical cost of three course meal for two with wine: £30.
**CARDS:** Visa and Access.

*At the time of going to press a change of landlords was in progress so some things may have altered.*

*The Restaurant which overlooks the seating provided outside and the river beyond was totally refurbished and extended in 1990.*

*Music is supplied by background tapes and the juke box has a decent selection of music. Dogs and children welcome.*

*Bed and breakfast at reasonable rates. Mostly en-suite rooms with TV and coffee/tea making facilities. Two day breaks available. Details on request.*

# COLTISHALL
## THE RED LION     TEL: (01603) 737402

### 4 MILES TO WROXHAM - 45 MINUTES

**MOORINGS:** These are plentiful and side on. There is no charge for the first 24 hours. Turn left at the top of the staithe, walk past the small parade of shops in the village and you will find the pub 400 yards down the road almost opposite the church. Torches required at night.

| | |
|---|---|
| **SUMMER:** | 11 to 3 and 5 to 11 |
| **WINTER:** | 11 to 3 and 5 to 11 |
| **SUNDAY:** | 12 to 3 and 7 to 10.30 |
| **BEERS:** | Old Speckled Hen, Abbot Ale, Flowers Original, Adnams, Couteshall Weaselpis, Brakspears, Boddingtons, Guinness & Murphys |
| **LAGERS:** | Heineken and Stella Artois |
| **CIDERS:** | Addlestons Cask Conditioned |
| **SPECIALITIES:** | Homecured Norfolk Ham. Local Trout. Fresh Cromer Crab. A La Carte menu. Separate Bar meals and lunchtime "specials". |
| **SUNDAY LUNCH:** | Roasts and Main menu available. |
| **BAR MEALS:** | Noon to 2 and 6.30 to 9.30  (Last Orders 2 pm and 9.30 pm) |

**DINING FACILITIES:** Seating for 60. Noon to 2 and 6.30 to 9.30 (Last Orders 2 pm and 9.30 pm). Typical cost of three course meal for two with wine: £25.
**CARDS:** Access, Visa, Switch and Eurocard.

*A quaint split level pub which was originally three Alms Houses and a very small beer house dating back to the 14th Century.*

*An interesting collection of Broadland photographs complements the unique character of this inviting hostelry where families are sure of good food and a warm welcome. Dogs are allowed, although not in the new "play" garden to the side.*

*The knowledge that the pub boasts seventeen consecutive entries in the "Good Beer Guide" will lure the traditional beer drinkers even if they failed to take note of one of the beers mentioned above which is brewed exclusively for the Red Lion!*

# WROXHAM

## THE CASTLE   TEL: (01603) 782588

**4 MILES FROM COLTISHALL - 45 MINUTES**
**1 MILE TO WROXHAM BRIDGE - 10 MINUTES**

**MOORINGS:** Approximately four side on to your right as you near Wroxham Bridge. No fees and the pub is a three minute walk away over the small common, bearing right over the railway bridge. Torches required at night.

| | |
|---|---|
| **SUMMER:** | All day |
| **WINTER:** | All day |
| **SUNDAY:** | 12 to 3 and 7 to 10.30 |
| **BEERS:** | Directors, John Smiths, Marstons, Courage, Guinness and Beamish. |
| **LAGERS:** | Fosters and Kronenbough 1664 |
| **CIDERS:** | Strongbow |
| **SPECIALITIES:** | Fifteen varieties of Omelette - or choose your own. Full breakfasts from 8.30 am - £2.85 (1994). |
| **SUNDAY LUNCH:** | Roast of the day - £4.25 (1994) |
| **BAR MEALS:** | Noon to 2 and 6 to 10 (Last Orders 2 pm and 9.30 pm) |

**DINING FACILITIES:** Seating for 16. Times as above. Typical cost of three course meal for two with wine: £15.
**CARDS:** Cheque with bankers card.

*The only "pub" in Wroxham, has been renovated to a very high standard. Chintz furnishings, pink and blue plates, farming implements and light background music add to the tasteful surroundings, as does the open log fireplace.*

*There are two bars with pool and darts available in the public bar where dogs are allowed. Children are welcome, there are large gardens to the rear and wheelchair access is provided. Take away food.*

*Live music every other Sunday, a flower for every lady who eats here, a pizza oven in the bar and a raft race in February! What next?*

# WROXHAM BRIDGE

## KINGS HEAD HOTEL     TEL: (01603) 782429

### 5 MILES FROM COLTISHALL - 1 HOUR
### 5 MILES TO HORNING - 1 HOUR

**MOORINGS:** On the Coltishall side of the bridge, on your right at the "bottom of the garden". There is no charge if you use the facilities. Alternatively - walk over from various boat yard moorings on the Wroxham side.

| | |
|---|---|
| **SUMMER:** | All day |
| **WINTER:** | All day |
| **SUNDAY:** | 12 to 3 and 7 to 10.30 |

**BEERS:** Directors, Ruddles County, Websters and John Smith

**LAGERS:** Carlsberg, Fosters and Kronenberg

**CIDERS:** Strongbow, Woodpecker and Scrumpy Jack

**SPECIALITIES:** Good selection of Chef's Fayre all with fresh vegetables. From £3.75p.

**SUNDAY LUNCH:** £9.99 per head (1994) Carvery all day

**BAR MEALS:** Noon to 9 pm in the Riverside Bar Bar-B-Q's - weather permitting.

**DINING FACILITIES:** Seating for 100. Noon to 2 and 6.30 to 9.30 (Last Orders 1.45 pm and 9.30 pm). Typical cost of three course meal for two with wine: £27.

**CARDS:** Access, Visa, Diners and Amex.

*This is a large hotel with all facilities and therefore has something for everyone. Friendly service in an informal atmosphere. Music is provided by background tapes and there is a juke box in the Village Bar. The non-smoking Carvery, where the two course special is £6.99, is attractive and roomy and the Conservatory overlooks the river.*

*Live entertainment several nights a week in the Waterfront Room. There is a childrens' room, play area and large gardens where dogs are welcome.*

*If you'd like to try your luck at fishing (especially pike) the hotel offers special holidays, which are all inclusive, from 1st November to 16th March.*

# HORNING

*3 d/12*

## THE SWAN HOTEL  TEL: (01692) 630316

**5 MILES FROM WROXHAM - 1 HOUR**
**3 MILES TO RANWORTH - 30 MINUTES**

**MOORINGS:** Approximately 10 side on. There is no charge and the hotel is across the lawns.

| | |
|---|---|
| **SUMMER:** | All day |
| **WINTER:** | All day |
| **SUNDAY:** | 12 to 3 and 7 to 10.30 |

| | |
|---|---|
| **BEERS:** | Whitbread Best, Boddingtons, Guinness, Murphys and Guests |
| **LAGERS:** | Stella Artois and Heineken |
| **CIDERS:** | Woodpecker and Strongbow |

| | |
|---|---|
| **SPECIALITIES:** | Oriental Prawns. Chicken Balti. Vegetarians and Childrens menu |

**SUNDAY LUNCH:** Roasts - £4.95 (1994)

**BAR MEALS:** 11.30 am to 10 pm. Noon to 10 pm on Sundays.

**DINING FACILITIES:** Seating for 44. 7 to 9.30 (Last Orders 9.15 pm). Typical cost of three course meal for two with wine: £25.
**CARDS:** Access and Visa.

*Long and rambling this hotel was built in 1897. Generous seating is provided in the gardens which front onto the river and there are Bar-B-Q's in the summer months.*

*You can settle yourself anywhere for a snack - although an off-set dining room is offered together with a small no-smoking area. Pool and darts are provided and there is a games area together with a room for "Ladies and Children". Small dogs are allowed in the vicinity of the inner balcony and the gardens. Family entertainment is regularly organised.*

*En Suite rooms are available for bed and breakfast. Please telephone ahead for details.*

# HORNING

## THE FERRY INN   TEL: (01692) 630259

**5 1/2  MILES FROM WROXHAM - 1 HOUR
2 1/2 MILES TO RANWORTH - 30 MINUTES**

**MOORINGS:**   There are a number of moorings all around Horning proper but outside the pub there is room for about 15 side on.  A charge of £2.50 is levied.

| | |
|---|---|
| **SUMMER:** | All day (June to September) |
| **WINTER:** | 11 to 2.30 and 7 to 11 |
| **SUNDAY:** | 12 to 3 and 7 to 10.30 |

| | |
|---|---|
| **BEERS:** | John Smiths, Theakstons Best, Guinness, Websters, and Directors |
| **LAGERS:** | Carlsberg, Holsten and Fosters |
| **CIDERS:** | Woodpecker and Strongbow |

**SPECIALITIES:**   Carvery roast lunch and evening. Vegetarian dishes.

**SUNDAY LUNCH:**   Main course - £4.50.  Sweets - £2.

**BAR MEALS:**   Noon to 9 pm. (Cold food available between 2 pm and 7 pm.)

**DINING FACILITIES:**  Seating for 50 in the dining area.  Meal times as above.  Typical cost of two course meal for two with wine:  £20.

**CARDS:**  Diners, Access, Visa and Amex.

*Built on the site of Monks' Mead House in 1840, bombed in 1941 and gutted in 1965 due to a thatch fire this is one of Broadlands better known pubs and can certainly lay claim to being one of the most photographed!*

*Coaching lamps, copper jugs and an open fireplace enhance the atmosphere and although there is no music, a large games room is available complete with jukeboxes. There are rides for the children and there is a "child free" area in the lounge.  You are requested not to smoke in the dining part of the pub.*

*A covered patio area stretches down to the river and the wide doors and lack of steps make the Inn convenient for those with wheelchairs.*

# RANWORTH

**MALTSTERS**   TEL: (01603) 270241

**3 MILES FROM HORNING - 30 MINUTES**
**1 MILE TO ANT MOUTH - 10 MINUTES**
**2 MILES TO THURNE MOUTH - 20 MINUTES**
**5 MILES TO UPTON DYKE - 45 MINUTES**

**MOORINGS:**  These are plentiful and stern on.  There is no charge for the first 24 hours and the distance to the pub is 100/200 yards - opposite the Granary stores and restaurant.

| | |
|---|---|
| **SUMMER:** | All day  (June to August) |
| **WINTER:** | 11 to 2.30 and 7 to 11 |
| **SUNDAY:** | 12 to 3 and 7 to 10.30 |
| | |
| **BEERS:** | Theakstons Best, Websters, Norwich Bitter and Mild |
| **LAGERS:** | Holsten, Carlsberg and Fosters |
| **CIDERS:** | Strongbow |
| | |
| **SPECIALITIES:** | Lincolnshire sausages. Vegetable Lasagne.  Homemade fruit pie. |
| | |
| **SUNDAY LUNCH:** | £4.50 per head (1994). |
| | |
| **BAR MEALS:** | 11.30 to 2 and 6.30 to 9  (Last Orders 2 pm and 9 pm) |

**DINING FACILITIES:**  Seating for 40.  11.30 to 2  and 6.30 to 9 (Last Orders 2 pm and 9 pm).  Typical cost of two course meal for two with wine: £18.
**CARDS:**  Access, Visa and Diners.

Extensive refurbishments during 1989 have not detracted from the charm of this lovely old pub which was built in 1762.  The split-level bar, lounge and dining area are well decorated with comfortable seating in a relaxing atmosphere.

Background music is in keeping with the setting and a childrens room lies behind the old Ship's Prow which has been lovingly reconstructed at the rear of the pub.

Ranworth itself boasts one of Broadlands most beautiful churches and if you climb to the top you are promised an excellent view.  Here, also, is Broadlands Conservation Centre and Nature Trail.

# UPTON DYKE

## THE WHITE HORSE   TEL: (01493) 750696

**5 MILES FROM RANWORTH - 45 MINUTES**
**2 MILES FROM THURNE MOUTH - 20 MINUTES**
**1 MILE TO ACLE BRIDGE - 10 MINUTES**

**MOORINGS:** A 3 m.p.h. limit to the head of the dyke which has a turning basin at the end. Room for 10 boats moored side on along the bank. Distance to the pub is a ten minute walk through the village. Torches useful at night.

| | |
|---|---|
| **SUMMER:** | All day |
| **WINTER:** | All day |
| **SUNDAY:** | 12 to 3 and 7 to 10.30 |
| | |
| **BEERS:** | Chalk Hill, Fullers, Old Tackle and Great Eastern (all local brews), Murphys, Tetley and Adnams |
| **LAGERS:** | Carlsberg and Grolsch |
| **CIDERS:** | Stowford Press |
| | |
| **SPECIALITIES:** | Continental food nights. Childrens menu. Vegetarian dishes. |
| | |
| **SUNDAY LUNCH:** | Roast and sweet - £4.95 (1994) |
| | |
| **BAR MEALS:** | 11 to 3 and 6 to 9 (Last Orders 2.30 pm and 9 pm) |

**DINING FACILITIES:** Seating for 16 and one at the piano! Times as for bar meals. Typical cost of two course meal for two with wine: £20.
**CARDS:** Cheque with bankers card.

*Built in 1824, this pub became a Freehouse recently. Not previously featured in this Guide, it should have been, for there is never a dull moment.*

*Truly traditional decor right down to the wood burning stoves and the snug with its grandmother clock. Read about the "Drinker's Lament". In the raised restaurant you may well feel that time has stood still - but not for obvious reasons!*

*Darts are provided together with live music every Thursday night and fish and chips on Fridays. Children and dogs are welcome and there is a pretty L-shaped garden to the rear. A free taxi service is available back to your boat.*

# ACLE BRIDGE 31/12

## THE BRIDGE    TEL: (01493) 750288

*New Year Booked 2pm*

**1 MILE FROM UPTON DYKE - 10 MINUTES**
**2 MILES TO STOKESBY - 20 MINUTES**

**MOORINGS:** These are numerous on both sides of the river. There is no charge unless you moor on certain areas west of the bridge in which case a small fee overnight is requested. Distance to pub is 75/200 yards. Torches may be useful at night.

| | |
|---|---|
| **SUMMER:** | All day (late May to September) |
| **WINTER:** | 11 to 2.30 and 7 to 11 |
| **SUNDAY:** | 12 to 3 and 7 to 10.30 |
| **BEERS:** | Theakstons, Ruddles County, Websters, Guinness and Norwich Bitter |
| **LAGERS:** | Carlsberg, Fosters and Holsten |
| **CIDERS:** | Woodpecker and Strongbow |
| **SPECIALITIES:** | Home cooked roasts and pies Vegetarian meals. |
| **SUNDAY LUNCH:** | £4.50 per head. Children £3.00 |
| **BAR MEALS:** | Noon to 2 and 7 to 9 (Last Orders 2 pm and 9 pm) |

**DINING FACILITIES:** Seating for 50 anywhere in pub and in Dining Area. Times as above. Typical cost of two course meal for two with wine: £20.
**CARDS:** Access and Visa.

*A warm and inviting inn, tastefully decorated and with enough staff to cope during busy times. As Acle Bridge is a fairly large "beginning and ending" area there is usually the odd hilarious tale to tell or be told. Boating enthusiasts will find a sympathetic ear in the staff.*

*No smoking in the Dining Area but plenty of seating is available in the pub. Cold food every afternoon in Summer. Large gardens, dogs welcome and play areas for children provided inside and out.*

*Pleasant background music is played and good facilities for the disabled are available.*
*Don't forget to ask about the legend of the Bridge.*

# STOKESBY

## THE FERRY INN  TEL: (01493) 751096

### 2 MILES FROM ACLE BRIDGE - 20 MINUTES
### 2 MILES TO TUNSTALL - 20 MINUTES

**MOORINGS:** On the pub side of the river there is room for 20 or so boats. A small fee for 24 hours is collected downstream by local residents. Distance to the pub is 50/200 yards. Keep an eye on rise and fall of the river.

| | |
|---|---|
| **SUMMER:** | All day |
| **WINTER:** | 11 to 3 and 7 to 11 |
| **SUNDAY:** | 12 to 3 and 7 to 10.30 |
| **BEERS:** | Whitbread Bitter and Mild, Adnams Flowers, Boddingtons and Murphys |
| **LAGERS:** | Heineken and Stella Artois |
| **CIDERS:** | Olde English and Stowford Press |
| **SPECIALITIES:** | Chef's home made dishes using fresh local produce and vegetables. Childrens and Vegetarians menu. |
| **SUNDAY LUNCH:** | Roasts, plus 40 dishes to choose from. |
| **BAR MEALS:** | 11 to 2.30 and 6 to 9.30 (Last Orders 2.15 pm and 9.15 pm) |

**DINING FACILITIES:** Seating anywhere. Times as above. Typical cost of two course meal for two with wine: £13.

**CARDS:** Cheque with bankers card.

*Long, low and rambling with a pretty garden and patio area overlooking the river this is a genuine Olde Worlde Inn with one oak-beamed bar full of brassware, copper, pictures and general bric a brac.*

*The background music is not overpowering and there is a large comfortable lounge and family room.*

*The Inn is now Egon Ronay listed and, indeed, the food on offer is well worth a visit.*

*In Stokesby itself there is a workshop specialising in candle making and two miles away by road are the wildlife gardens of Thrigby Hall.*

# TUNSTALL

## STRACEY ARMS    TEL: (01493) 651311

**2 MILES FROM STOKESBY FERRY - 20 MINUTES**
**8 MILES TO GREAT YARMOUTH - 1 1/2 HOURS**

**MOORINGS:** Plentiful and side on just outside the pub which is on your right as you go downstream to Great Yarmouth. There is no charge. Torches useful at night.

| | |
|---|---|
| **SUMMER:** | All day |
| **WINTER:** | 11 to 3 and 7 to 11 |
| **SUNDAY:** | 12 to 3 and 7 to 10.30 |

| | |
|---|---|
| **BEERS:** | Whitbread Best and Mild, Tetleys and Murphys |
| **LAGERS:** | Castlemaine XXXX, Stella and Carlsberg |
| **CIDERS:** | Red Rock |

| | |
|---|---|
| **SPECIALITIES:** | Half chicken. Mixed Grill. Fish. Childrens Menu. Liqueur coffee. |
| **SUNDAY LUNCH:** | £4.25 (1994) |
| **BAR MEALS:** | Noon to 2.30 and 7 to 10 (Last Orders 2.15 pm and 9.45 pm) |

**DINING FACILITIES:** Seating anywhere in the pub. Times as above. Typical cost of a two course meal with wine: £14.
**CARDS:** Cheque with bankers card.

*A popular establishment with families this pub has recently been refurbished. Pleasant background music, darts and pool are provided.*

*There is one long bar with a games room at the end. A raised stage is provided for entertainment and, at present, there is live music every Sunday night.*

*Children are welcome but no dogs are allowed in the pub.*

*Round in the smaller bar try your luck with the Putting Game!*

# GREAT YARMOUTH

## SUSPENSION BRIDGE TAVERN   TEL: (01493) 857151

### 8 MILES FROM TUNSTALL - 1 1/2 HOURS
### 4 MILES TO BREYDON WATER'S END - 30 MINUTES

**MOORINGS:** Around 100 in the Marina. 1994 charge was £8 from 10 am to 10 am. The Yacht Station charges in 1994 were £10 from 11 am to 11 am. The Tavern is on your right over Vauxhall Bridge.

| | |
|---|---|
| **SUMMER:** | All day |
| **WINTER:** | All day |
| **SUNDAY:** | 12 to 3 and 7 to 10.30 |
| **BEERS:** | Whitbread Best and Mild, IPA, Boddingtons, Murphys, Flowers and Guest Beers |
| **LAGERS:** | Heineken and Stella Artois |
| **CIDERS:** | Strongbow and Scrumpy Jack |
| **SPECIALITIES:** | Duck a l'orange.  Jam Roly Poly. |
| **SUNDAY LUNCH:** | £4.95 - Choice of three Roasts |
| **BAR MEALS:** | Noon to 2.30 and 6 to 10  (Last Orders 2.30 pm and 9.30 pm) |

**DINING FACILITIES:** Seating for 24 and anywhere in pub. Times as above.  Typical cost of two course meal for two with wine: £20.

**CARDS:** Cheque with bankers card.

*Renovated to a very high standard since the last edition with excellent facilities for the disabled. Children and dogs welcome.*

*Friendly service in congenial surroundings with pleasant background music. The menu is extensive and caters for all tastes and there is a restaurant licence.  Perhaps one of the best  aspects is the raised balcony area where you can sit and watch the river traffic as you dine.*

*Live entertainment is provided on Saturday nights all year round and also mid week in the summer.*

# THE RIVERS YARE AND CHET - DISTANCES AND TIMINGS

## BERNEY ARMS MILL (BREYDON WATER) TO NORWICH YACHT STATION

BERNEY ARMS MILL TO MOUTH OF NEW CUT = 2 MILES - 20 MINUTES
MOUTH OF NEW CUT TO REEDHAM (THE LORD NELSON) = 2 1/2 MILES - 25 MINUTES
REEDHAM TO LODDON (THE SWAN, THE ANGEL) = 5 MILES - 45 MINUTES
REEDHAM TO CANTLEY (THE RED HOUSE) = 4 MILES - 30 MINUTES
LODDON TO CANTLEY = 5 MILES - 45 MINUTES
CANTLEY TO BUCKENHAM FERRY (THE BEAUCHAMP ARMS) = 3 MILES - 30 MINUTES
BUCKENHAM FERRY TO ROCKLAND BROAD (THE NEW INN) = 2 MILES - 30 MINUTES
ROCKLAND BROAD TO BRUNDALL OR SURLINGHAM STAITHE (WHITE HORSE, COLDHAM HALL)
= 3 MILES - 30 MINUTES
BRUNDALL OR SURLINGHAM STAITHE TO SURLINGHAM (FERRY HOUSE) = 1 MILE - 15 MINUTES
SURLINGHAM TO THORPE (THE KINGS ARMS, THE RUSHCUTTERS) = 5 MILES - 45 MINUTES
THORPE TO NORWICH YACHT STATION (THE BRIDGE HOUSE, THE RED LION) = 2 MILES - 30 MINUTES

## NORWICH YACHT STATION TO BERNEY ARMS MILL (BREYDON WATER)

NORWICH YACHT STATION (THE BRIDGE HOUSE, THE RED LION) TO THORPE = 2 MILES - 30 MINUTES
THORPE (THE KINGS ARMS, THE RUSHCUTTERS) TO SURLINGHAM = 5 MILES - 45 MINUTES
SURLINGHAM (FERRY HOUSE) TO BRUNDALL OR SURLINGHAM STAITHE = 1 MILE - 15 MINUTES
BRUNDALL OR SURLINGHAM STAITHE (COLDHAM HALL, WHITE HORSE) TO ROCKLAND BROAD
= 3 MILES - 30 MINUTES
ROCKLAND BROAD (THE NEW INN) TO BUCKENHAM FERRY = 2 MILES - 30 MINUTES
BUCKENHAM FERRY (BEAUCHAMP ARMS) TO CANTLEY = 3 MILES - 30 MINUTES
CANTLEY (THE RED HOUSE) TO LODDON = 5 MILES - 45 MINUTES
CANTLEY TO REEDHAM = 4 MILES - 30 MINUTES
LODDON (THE SWAN INN, THE ANGEL) TO REEDHAM = 5 MILES - 45 MINUTES
REEDHAM (THE LORD NELSON) TO MOUTH OF NEW CUT = 2 1/2 MILES - 25 MINUTES
MOUTH OF NEW CUT TO BERNEY ARMS MILL = 2 MILES - 20 MINUTES

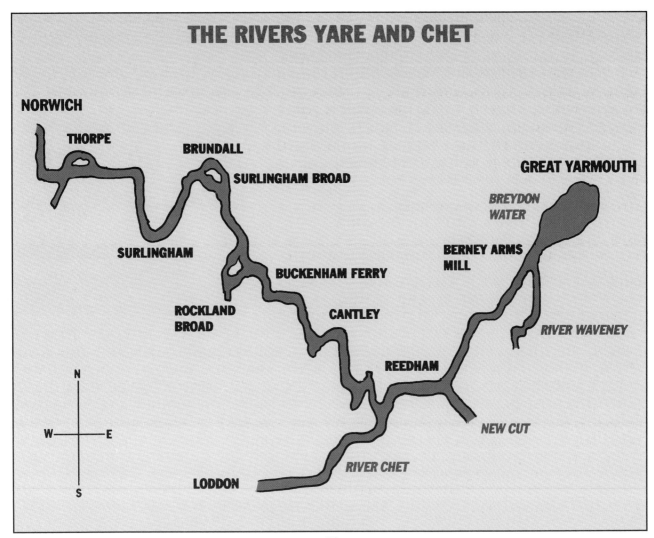

# THE RIVERS YARE AND CHET

NORWICH

THORPE

BRUNDALL

SURLINGHAM BROAD

GREAT YARMOUTH

*BREYDON WATER*

SURLINGHAM

BUCKENHAM FERRY

BERNEY ARMS MILL

ROCKLAND BROAD

CANTLEY

*RIVER WAVENEY*

N

REEDHAM

W — E

*NEW CUT*

*RIVER CHET*

LODDON

S

CROSSING BREYDON WATER IS NOT AS DAUNTING AS IT LOOKS FROM MOST MAPS. ALWAYS CROSS AT LOW TIDES. YOUR ANNUAL TIDE TABLE WILL TELL YOU WHEN THESE ARE. WHEN GOING UNDER BREYDON BRIDGE TAKE CARE TO STEER UNDER THE RED AND WHITE STRIPED TRIANGLES WHICH POINT DOWN TO THE RIVER. IF THREE RED LIGHTS SHOW ON THE BRIDGE KEEP TO THE EXTREME RIGHT HAND CHANNEL. FROM GREAT YARMOUTH TO BERNEY ARMS MILL KEEP BETWEEN THE POSTS AS FOLLOWS:

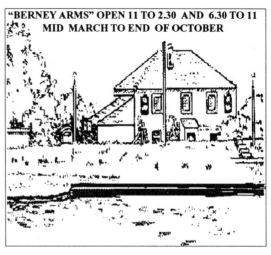

"BERNEY ARMS" OPEN 11 TO 2.30 AND 6.30 TO 11 MID MARCH TO END OF OCTOBER

**RED ON YOUR LEFT (PORT) HAND SIDE.**
**GREEN OR BLACK WITH A WHITE TOP ON YOUR**
**RIGHT (STARBOARD) HAND SIDE.**
**REVERSE THE ABOVE IF COMING TOWARDS YARMOUTH.**

BERNEY ARMS MILL IS THE TALLEST IN NORFOLK, IN FULL WORKING ORDER AND CAN BE VISITED, AS CAN THE SURROUNDING MARSHES THAT BELONG TO THE R.S.P.B. ONCE PAST THE NEW CUT (A SHORT ROUTE TO THE RIVER WAVENEY) REEDHAM CAN BE SEEN. FURTHER ALONG YOU SHOULD WATCH OUT FOR REEDHAM CAR FERRY. THIS IS THE LAST WORKING CHAIN FERRY IN EAST ANGLIA. IF YOU ARE NOT GOING TO LODDON YOU WILL SHORTLY ARRIVE AT CANTLEY WHERE THE FIRST SUGAR BEET FACTORY TO BE BUILT IN THIS COUNTRY IS STILL IN USE. THE RIVER FROM HERE TO THORPE, NEAR NORWICH, IS WIDE AND PLEASANT WITH MANY INTERESTING PUBS ON THE WAY. ONE OF THOSE NOT FEATURED IN THIS EDITION, SINCE IT WAS UNDERGOING EXTENSIVE RENOVATIONS AT THE TIME OF GOING TO PRESS, IS THE "WOODS END TAVERN". THORPE BRIDGES ARE 6' AND 6.2" AT HIGH WATER.

IF YOU ARE GOING TO LODDON YOU WILL TRAVEL DOWN THE RIVER CHET WHICH IS 3 1/2 MILES LONG. THIS STRETCH HAS A 3 M.P.H. SPEED LIMIT AND CARE IS NEEDED. LODDON IS A PRETTY MARKET TOWN WITH THE CHURCH OF THE HOLY TRINITY AT ITS CENTRE.

# REEDHAM

## LORD NELSON
**TEL: (01493) 701239**

**4 1/2 MILES FROM BERNEY ARMS MILL - 45 MINUTES
5 MILES TO LODDON - 45 MINUTES
4 MILES TO CANTLEY - 30 MINUTES**

**MOORINGS:** Six to eight side on. Double mooring permitted. There is no charge if you are patrons. If not, £5 after 6 pm. Distance to the pub is 25/50 yards. Please keep an eye on rise and fall of the river if moored overnight.

| | |
|---|---|
| **SUMMER:** | All day (Easter to September) |
| **WINTER:** | 11 to 3 and 6 to 11 |
| **SUNDAY:** | 12 to 3 and 7 to 10.30 |
| **BEERS:** | Abbott, Rayments, IPA, Tartan, Guinness, Whitbread Mild and Guests Ales |
| **LAGERS:** | Kronenberg and Harp |
| **CIDERS:** | Woodpecker and Dry Blackthorn |
| **SPECIALITIES:** | T-Bone steak. Garlic Prawns. Childrens menu. Home made pies. |
| **SUNDAY LUNCH:** | £4.95 main course (1994) |
| **BAR MEALS:** | Noon to 2 and 6.30 to 9 (Last Orders 2 pm and 9 pm) |

**DINING FACILITIES:** Seating for 42. Times as for bar meals. Typical cost of three course meal for two with wine: £25
**CARDS:** Cheque with bankers card.

*Not featured since the first edition this pub was entirely renovated and reopened in May 1993.*

*There is one large bar with a pleasant dining room to your left which overlooks the river.*

*Children and dogs are welcome and there are open fires and musical evenings.*

*Bed and breakfast is available. Please telephone ahead for details.*

*It is from outside this pub that the local "fun" bus for Pettits Farm has its pick-up and return point.*

# REEDHAM

## THE SHIP     (01493) 700287

**4 1/2 MILES FROM BERNEY ARMS MILL - 45 MINUTES
1 MILE TO REEDHAM FERRY - 15 MINUTES
4 MILES TO CANTLEY - 30 MINUTES**

**MOORINGS:** Three, side on, by the pub which is very near the railway bridge. No charge and entrance is via a walk through the gardens. Please keep an eye on rise and fall of river if moored overnight.

| | |
|---|---|
| **SUMMER:** | 11 to 2.30 and 6 to 11 |
| **WINTER:** | 11 to 2.30 and 6 to 11 |
| **SUNDAY:** | 12 to 2.30 and 7 to 10.30 |

**BEERS:** Adnams, Stones, Worthington Best, Toby, Caffreys and Guinness

**LAGERS:** Carling Black Label, Tennents Pilsner

**CIDERS:** Dry Blackthorn and Autumn Gold

**SPECIALITIES:** Different daily specials. Childrens menu from £1.95

**SUNDAY LUNCH:** Noon to 2.30. Evenings: 7 to 9 pm.

**BAR MEALS:** 11 to 2.30 and 6.30 to 9.30 (Last Orders 2.30 pm and 9.30 pm)

**DINING FACILITIES:** Seating for 20. 11 to 2.30 and 6.30 to 9.30 (Last Orders 2.30 pm and 9.30 pm) Typical cost of three course meal for two with wine: £25.

**CARDS:** Cheque with bankers card.

# REEDHAM FERRY

## REEDHAM FERRY INN     (01493) 700429

**1 MILE FROM REEDHAM - 15 MINUTES
4 MILES TO LODDON - 45 MINUTES
3 MILES TO CANTLEY - 20 MINUTES**

**MOORINGS:** Plentiful, side on, at the pub side of the river. £5 is charged. Distance to the pub is 100/200 yards. Again, please keep an eye on rise and fall of the river if moored overnight.

| | |
|---|---|
| **SUMMER:** | 11 to 3 and 6.30 to 11 |
| **WINTER:** | 11 to 2.30 and 7 to 11 |
| **SUNDAY:** | 12 to 3 and 7 to 10.30 |

**BEERS:** Wherry. Adnams, Youngers Mild and Tartan, Export and Murphys

**LAGERS:** Becks, Tuborg Gold and Carlsberg

**CIDERS:** Autumn Gold

**SPECIALITIES:** Seafood and Steaks. Norfolk wine.

**SUNDAY LUNCH:** Main menu available

**BAR MEALS:** Noon to 2 and 7 to 10 (Last Orders 2 pm and 10 pm)

**DINING FACILITIES:** Seating for 28. 12 to 3 and 6.30 to 9.30 (Last Orders 2 pm and 9.30 pm). Typical cost of three course meal for two with wine. £25.

**CARDS:** Access and Visa.

# LODDON

## THE SWAN INN    TEL: (01508) 520239

**5 MILES FROM REEDHAM - 45 MINUTES**
**5 MILES TO CANTLEY - 45 MINUTES**

**MOORINGS:** Plentiful at the Staithe - mostly stern on.
There is no charge. Turn left by the Bridge and the Swan
is a three minute stroll away, opposite the Church.

| | |
|---|---|
| **SUMMER:** | 11 to 3 and 6.30 to 11 |
| **WINTER:** | 11 to 3 and 6.30 to 11 |
| **SUNDAY:** | 12 to 3 and 7 to 10.30 |

**BEERS:**    Whitbread Best and Mild, Marstons
Pedigree, Boddingtons, Murphys,
Old Speckled Hen, Fullers Chiswick
and 6X

**LAGERS:**    Stella Artois and Heineken
**CIDERS:**    Bulmers Old Original

**SPECIALITIES:**    Steaks. Very hot curries and Chilli's.
Salmon steaks in Puff Pastry.

**SUNDAY LUNCH:**    £4.00 per head (1994)

**BAR MEALS:**    Noon to 2.30 and 7 to 10 (Last
Orders 2.30 pm and 9.30 pm)

**DINING FACILITIES:** Seating for 28. 7 to 11 (Last Orders
9.30 pm). Typical cost of three course meal for two with
wine: £30.
**CARDS:** Access and Visa.

*This is a delightful 17th/18th Century Coaching Inn. The decor is superb and it is well worth a visit to the restaurant and to the lounge area which lies at one end of the long bar.*

*There is a pool table and video machines in the upstairs bar and plenty of seating outside for those hot days. Children and dogs are welcome.*

*Music is provided by background tapes and a juke box. A sale and market is held every alternate Monday in the pub car park.*

*It is hoped that bed and breakfast will be offered within the next year or so. Take away food.*

# LODDON

## THE ANGEL    TEL: (01508) 520763

**5 MILES FROM REEDHAM - 45 MINUTES**
**5 MILES TO CANTLEY - 45 MINUTES**

**MOORINGS:**    Plentiful at the Staithe - mostly stern on. There is no charge.  Turn left by the bridge and the pub is a three minute stroll away - on the left just past the church.

| | |
|---|---|
| **SUMMER:** | 11 to 3 and 7 to 11 |
| **WINTER:** | 11 to 3 and 7 to 11 |
| **SUNDAY:** | 12 to 3 and 7 to 10.30 |

| | |
|---|---|
| **BEERS:** | Worthington, Toby and Mild |
| **LAGERS:** | Tennents Extra and Black Label |
| **CIDERS:** | Dry Blackthorn |

**SPECIALITIES:**    Farmhouse Chicken Pie.  Scampi. Pate.  Childrens Menu.

**SUNDAY LUNCH:**    £3.95 (1994)

**BAR MEALS:**    11 to 2.30 and 7 to 10 (Last Orders 2.30 pm and 9.30 pm)

**DINING FACILITIES:**  Seating anywhere in the pub.  11 to 2.30 and 7 to 10 (Last Orders 2.30 pm and 9.30 pm).  Typical cost of a main meal for two with wine:  £10.
**CARDS:**    Cheque with bankers card.

*Not previously featured, this is the oldest pub in the village.*

*There are three bars with two being on split levels. In the dining room there is an unusual thatched "roof" to the bar area. During partial renovations over twenty years ago an ex-landlord requested that his initials be carved for posterity. On looking closely at some of the beams these can still be deciphered.*

*The original stables and Smoke House can be found at the rear of the pub together with a patio and garden.  Dogs are welcome, a pool table is provided and there is a separate family room.*

# CANTLEY

## THE RED HOUSE    TEL: (01493) 700801

**4 MILES FROM REEDHAM - 30 MINUTES**
**5 MILES FROM LODDON - 45 MINUTES**
**3 MILES TO BUCKENHAM FERRY - 30 MINUTES**

**MOORINGS:** There are between 20 to 30 side on. There was a small charge for overnight collected by local farmers in 1994. Distance to the pub is 50/100 yards.

| | |
|---|---|
| **SUMMER:** | All day |
| **WINTER:** | 11 to 3 and 7 to 11 |
| **SUNDAY:** | 12 to 3 and 7 to 10.30 |
| **BEERS:** | Guinness, Keg Bitters, Mild and Real Ales |
| **LAGERS:** | Carlsberg and imported Grolsch on draught |
| **CIDERS:** | Addlestones and Gaymers Old English dry |
| **SPECIALITIES:** | Fresh home cooked meals. |
| **SUNDAY LUNCH:** | Not available at present |
| **BAR MEALS:** | Noon to 2 and 7 to 9 (Last Orders 1.45 pm and 8.45 pm) |

**DINING FACILITIES:** Seating anywhere in the pub. Times as above. Typical cost of a meal: £5.

**CARDS:** Cheque with bankers card.

*This sprawling Freehouse with its fruit machines, juke boxes and background music, a dart board and pool table changed hands again in 1994.*

*A beer garden runs alongside the pub and there are seats outside overlooking the river. Small children are safe from the river in a protected play area and dogs are welcome - "so long as they don't bite".
Is there something wrong with that clock on the wall???*

*The Legend outside reads: "Good wine, a friend, or being dry, or lest we should be by and by, or any other reason why".*

# BUCKENHAM FERRY

## BEAUCHAMP ARMS    TEL: (01508) 480247

**3 MILES FROM CANTLEY - 30 MINUTES**
**2 MILES TO ROCKLAND BROAD - 30 MINUTES**

**MOORINGS:** Either side of the pub will accommodate 40 comfortably side on and 50 if double moored. There is no charge and the distance to the pub is 25/50 yards. Torches may be useful if moored a little way from the pub.

| | |
|---|---|
| **SUMMER:** | All day (When trade demands) |
| **WINTER:** | 12 to 3 Saturdays only and 6 to 11 every night |
| **SUNDAY:** | 12 to 3 and 7 to 10.30 |
| **BEERS:** | Stones, M&B Mild, Murphys, Boddingtons, Wherry and Phoenix |
| **LAGERS:** | Carling, Tennants and Lamot |
| **CIDERS:** | Strongbow and Autumn Gold |
| **SPECIALITIES:** | Excellent roast duck. Steaks. Anything cooked if notice given. |
| **SUNDAY LUNCH:** | Carvery lunches at good value |
| **BAR MEALS:** | Noon to 2.30 and 7 to 10.30 (Last Orders 2 pm and 10 pm) |

**DINING FACILITIES:** Seating for 50. Noon to 3 and 7 to 11 (Last Orders 2 pm and 10 pm). Typical cost of three course meal for two with wine: £25.
**CARDS:** Cheque with bankers card.

*A large, friendly family pub with comfortable decor, good service and an extremely attractive restaurant. An interesting feature is the globe map of Norfolk.*

*A childrens room with games, books, crayons and video machines is provided together with an outside play area with swings and climbing frames. Guest bands visit at random.*

*Readers of past editions may recall the "love story" here. Whilst nothing has changed in that respect it is possible that by the time this book goes to print the couple involved will have sold the Beauchamp Arms. Let us hope it remains in good hands.*

# ROCKLAND BROAD

## THE NEW INN     TEL: (01508) 538395

**2 MILES FROM BUCKENHAM FERRY - 30 MINUTES**
**3 MILES TO BRUNDALL OR SURLINGHAM - 30 MINUTES**

**MOORINGS:** Room for about 15 boats stern on. There is no charge and the pub is 25/100 yards away. Torches may be useful at night.

| | |
|---|---|
| **SUMMER:** | 11 to 3 and 6 to 11 |
| **WINTER:** | 12 to 2.30 and 7 to 11 |
| **SUNDAY:** | 12 to 3 and 7 to 10.30 |

| | |
|---|---|
| **BEERS:** | Mild and Keg plus four Real Ales |
| **LAGERS:** | Carlsberg and Castlemaine |
| **CIDERS:** | Blackthorn |

**SPECIALITIES:**     Scampi. Steaks. Curries. Fish.

**SUNDAY LUNCH:**     Main menu available.

**BAR MEALS:**     12 to 2 and 7 to 9.30 (Last Orders 2 pm and 9.30 pm)

**DINING FACILITIES:** Seating for 34. Noon to 2 and 7 to 9.30 (Last Orders 2 pm and 9.30 pm). Typical cost of three course meal for two with wine: £20.
**CARDS:** Cheque with bankers card.

*An appealing and restful stopover in a quiet and peaceful backwater of the Broads. In 1994 the pub came under new ownership.*

*An extremely clean interior with historical pictures of the Broads round the walls. An attractive beer garden and various alterations have greatly enhanced this Inn. There is a no-smoking dining room.*

*A family room is provided and "take away food" is available.*

# SURLINGHAM STAITHE

## COLDHAM HALL TAVERN    TEL: (01508) 538591

**3 MILES FROM ROCKLAND BROAD - 30 MINUTES**
**1 MILE TO SURLINGHAM - 15 MINUTES**
**6 MILES TO THORPE - 1 HOUR**

**MOORINGS:** Approximately 25 stern on. There is no charge and the pub is 100/200 yards away.

| | |
|---|---|
| **SUMMER:** | 11.30 to 2.30 and 6.30 to 11 |
| **WINTER:** | 11.30 to 2.30 and 7 to 11 |
| **SUNDAY:** | 12 to 3 and 7 to 10.30 |

| | |
|---|---|
| **BEERS:** | Norwich Best and Mild, Ruddles, Guinness, Murphys, Bass and Tetley |
| **LAGERS:** | Carlsberg, Fosters, Holsten, Heineken and Stella Artois |
| **CIDERS:** | Bulmers and Scrumpy Jack |

| | |
|---|---|
| **SPECIALITIES:** | Large portions. Baked potatoes. Rack of lamb. Pasta. Chilli. |

| | |
|---|---|
| **SUNDAY LUNCH:** | Evening menu available |

| | |
|---|---|
| **BAR MEALS:** | Noon to 2 and 7 to 10 (Last Orders 2 pm and 9.30 pm) |

**DINING FACILITIES:** Seating for 100. Noon to 2 and 7 to 10 (Last Orders 2 pm and 9.30 pm). Typical cost of three course meal for two with wine: £26. Parties catered for.
**CARDS:** Access.

# SURLINGHAM

## THE FERRY HOUSE    TEL: (01508) 538227

**1 MILE FROM SURLINGHAM STAITHE - 15 MINUTES**
**5 MILES TO THORPE - 45 MINUTES**

**MOORINGS:** Room for about 30, side on, to your left alongside the pub. There is no charge.

| | |
|---|---|
| **SUMMER:** | 11 to 2.30 and 6.30 to 11 |
| **WINTER:** | Saturday evenings only from October to Easter. Lunchtimes as above. |
| **SUNDAY:** | 12 to 3 and 7 to 10.30 |

| | |
|---|---|
| **BEERS:** | Norwich Bitter and Mild, Websters Ruddles and Guest Beers |
| **LAGERS:** | Carlsberg |
| **CIDERS:** | Strongbow |

| | |
|---|---|
| **SPECIALITIES:** | Beef in Stout. Rump Bourguignonne. Chicken Chasseur. Bulgar Wheat and Walnut casserole. |

| | |
|---|---|
| **SUNDAY LUNCH:** | Main menu. Roasts in winter. |

| | |
|---|---|
| **BAR MEALS:** | Noon to 2.30 and 7 to 9 (Last Orders 2 pm and 9 pm) |

**DINING FACILITIES:** Seating for 20. No-smoking restaurant. Noon to 2.15 and 7 to 9.30 (Last Orders 2 pm and 9 pm). Typical cost of three course meal for two with wine: £25.
**CARDS:** Access and Visa ( 4 1/2% added)

# BRUNDALL

## THE WHITE HORSE          TEL: (01603) 716003

**3 MILES FROM ROCKLAND BROAD - 30 MINUTES**
**1 MILE TO SURLINGHAM - 15 MINUTES**
**6 MILES TO THORPE - 1 HOUR**

**MOORINGS:** Numerous boatyards are available. Distance is 400 yards over the railway bridge near to the Yare public house and up the hill. Torches required at night.

| | |
|---|---|
| **SUMMER:** | All day |
| **WINTER:** | All day |
| **SUNDAY:** | 12 to 3 and 7 to 10.30 |
| **BEERS:** | Websters, Guinness, IPA, Ruddles County, Budweiser, Theakstons and Guest Beers |
| **LAGERS:** | Holsten Export, Fosters, Carlsberg |
| **CIDERS:** | Strongbow |
| **SPECIALITIES:** | Fish and Chips. Pizzas. Spaghetti Bolognese. |
| **SUNDAY LUNCH:** | £4.95 (1994) |
| **BAR MEALS:** | Noon to 2 and 7 to 10 (Last Orders 2 pm and 9 pm) |

**DINING FACILITIES:** Seating for 24. Noon to 2 and 7 to 10 (Last Orders 2 pm and 9 pm) including Sunday evenings. Typical cost of two course meal for two: £12.
**CARDS:** Cheque with bankers card.

*This is one of the prettiest Inns in the area with its log fires and two oak-beamed bars full of brasses and pictures of horses. An appealing atmosphere is combined with speedy and cheerful service.*

*Background music and a juke box are supplied and there is a childrens room and play area, together with pool, darts and an outside seating area.*

*You can be a "hunter" or a "winner" depending on which bar you choose.*

*Your host also runs the Fish and Chip shop next door.*

# THORPE

## THE RUSHCUTTERS  TEL: (01603) 35403

### 6 MILES FROM BRUNDALL OR SURLINGHAM - 1 HOUR
### 2 MILES TO NORWICH - 30 MINUTES

**MOORINGS:** Room for about 15 boats moored side on. There is no charge and the pub is 25/50 yards away. Navigate carefully under the Bridges and check the tidal ebb and flow if stopping for long.

| | |
|---|---|
| **SUMMER:** | All day |
| **WINTER:** | 11 to 3 and 6 to 11 |
| **SUNDAY:** | 12 to 3 and 7 to 10.30 |

| | |
|---|---|
| **BEERS:** | Websters, Ruddles Best and County |
| **LAGERS:** | Carlsberg, Holsten and Fosters |
| **CIDERS:** | Strongbow |

| | |
|---|---|
| **SPECIALITIES:** | Tagliatelle. Cornish Pasty. Spotted Dick. Hot Chocolate Fudge Cake. |

| | |
|---|---|
| **SUNDAY LUNCH:** | Carvery £4.50 (1994). Children - £3 |

| | |
|---|---|
| **BAR MEALS:** | Noon to 2 and 7 to 9 (Last Orders 2 pm and 9 pm) |

**DINING FACILITIES:** Seating anywhere in pub. Times as above. Typical cost of three course meal for two with wine: £18.
**CARDS:** Visa, Access, Diners and Amex.

*A spacious hostelry where everything is provided for the family from pleasant background music to live music on Sunday nights, two pool tables and a childrens area offset from the games room.*

*The bars and parts of the dining areas overlook the river and there is a vast Patio area outside, complete with rides, from where you can watch the world go by.*

*In the 18th Century a rail crash resulted in the place being used as a temporary morgue. Before the Rushcutters was a public house it was a Coaching Inn and before that a Monastery. The ghost of a monk is still frequently seen!*

# THORPE

## THE KINGS HEAD
**TEL: (01603) 33540**

**6 MILES FROM BRUNDALL OR SURLINGHAM - 1 HOUR
2 MILES TO NORWICH - 30 MINUTES**

**MOORINGS:** Room for three side on outside the pub and plenty a little further down along the river bank. Carefully under either Bridge and watch the tides.

| | |
|---|---|
| **SUMMER:** | All day |
| **WINTER:** | All day |
| **SUNDAY:** | 12 to 3 and 7 to 10.30 |

**BEERS:** Specialising in traditional cask conditioned Ales. Changing selections of no less than eight are always available including local favourites.

**LAGERS:** Heineken and Stella Artois

**CIDERS:** Strongbow and Addlestones Cask

**SPECIALITIES:** Chef's "blackboard" dishes of the day. Fresh local seafood. Homecooked speciality pies.

**SUNDAY LUNCH:** Carvery from £4.95 plus main menu.

**BAR MEALS:** Noon to 2 and 6.30 to 9.30 (Last Orders 2 pm and 9.30 pm)

**DINING FACILITIES:** Seating anywhere in pub. Noon to 2 and 6.30 to 9.30 (Last Orders 2 pm and 9.30 pm). Typical cost of three course meal for two with wine: £20.

**CARDS:** Visa, Access, Switch and Eurocard.

*The sister pub to the Red Lion at Coltishall. The timber and brick interior complements the pleasant furnishings and the service is friendly yet unobtrusive in a relaxing atmosphere. Dogs and children welcome.*

*Secluded landscaped gardens slope to the river and are overlooked by the King's Room in which the Sunday carvery is served. This room can also be booked for private functions. Sunday lunchtime jazz sessions in the garden are a summer feature.*

*History tells us that the King's Head sustained slight damage from enemy action in 1944. The pub dates back to 1700 and has known over thirty Landlords.*

# NORWICH YACHT STATION

## THE RED LION   TEL: (01603) 623300

### 2 MILES FROM THORPE - 30 MINUTES

**MOORINGS:** Plentiful and side on in the Yacht Basin where there is a charge for 24 hours of £6.80 (1994). Walk over the bridge at the top of the basin and the pub is on your right, adjacent to the bridge.

| | |
|---|---|
| **SUMMER:** | 11 to 3 and 5 to 11 |
| **WINTER:** | 11 to 3 and 5 to 11 |
| **SUNDAY:** | 12 to 3 and 7 to 10.30 |
| | |
| **BEERS:** | Ruddles, Websters and Guinness |
| **LAGERS:** | Fosters, Carlsberg and Holsten Export |
| **CIDERS:** | Woodpecker and Strongbow |
| | |
| **SPECIALITIES:** | Suffolk Hot Pot.  Spotted Dick. |
| | |
| **SUNDAY LUNCH:** | Main course - £4.25 (1994) |
| | |
| **BAR MEALS:** | Noon to 2 and 7 to 9 (Last Orders 2 pm and 9 pm) |

**DINING FACILITIES:** Seating anywhere in the pub and also in the offset dining room. Noon to 2 and 7 to 9 (Last Orders 2 pm and 9 pm). Typical cost of two course meal for two with wine: £15.
**CARDS:** Visa and Access.

*With its elongated bar, wood panelled seats and chintz furniture this is one of the older type pubs. Pots, jugs, farming implements and old advertisements add to the authenticity.*

*Pinball, pool, darts and fruit machines are available and children are welcome.*

*A glass conservatory gives a pleasant aspect over the river and this in turn leads to outside seating on the Patio. There is also seating outside the front of the pub.*

*Beware of Aubrey the ghost who walks round in a brown suit and is known for throwing food out of the fridges!*

# NORWICH YACHT STATION

## THE BRIDGE HOUSE  TEL: (01603) 625701

### 2 MILES FROM THORPE - 30 MINUTES

**MOORINGS:** Plentiful and side on in the Yacht Basin where there is a charge for 24 hours of £6.80 (1994). Walk up to the top of the yacht basin and the pub is on your right opposite the bridge.

| | |
|---|---|
| **SUMMER:** | 11.30 to 2.30 and 5.30 to 11 |
| **WINTER:** | 11.30 to 2.30 and 5.30 to 11 |
| **SUNDAY:** | 12 to 3 and 7 to 10.30 |
| **BEERS:** | Whitbread Best, IPA, Tetley, Abbot, Bridge Bitter, Guinness and Murphys |
| **LAGERS:** | Labatts, Tenants Pilsner, Stella and Carlsberg Export |
| **CIDERS:** | Dry Blackthorn |
| **SPECIALITIES:** | Rump Steak. Cottage Pie. Omelettes. Light snacks and childrens menu. |
| **SUNDAY LUNCH:** | Main course - £3.95 (1994) |
| **BAR MEALS:** | Noon to 2 and 6 to 9  (Last Orders 2 pm and 9 pm) |

**DINING FACILITIES:** Seating anywhere in pub although there is a dining area.  Times as for bar meals.   Typical cost of three course meal for two with wine: £15.

**CARDS:**   Cheque with bankers card.

*Known as the Kings Arms until 1979 this is a lovely little pub with inglenook seating, oak beams and a large open fireplace with copper screens and bowls on its hearth.*

*If you stand at the brick and tiled bar you can be amused for quite a while by the up to date cartoons on the latest news billeted there.*

*Pleasant background music and a CD player are provided and children are welcome if dining with their parents.*

*An interesting history of the Bridge House appears on the back of their menus.*

# THE RIVER WAVENEY - DISTANCES AND TIMINGS

## BURGH CASTLE TO GELDESTON

BURGH CASTLE TO ST. OLAVES (THE BELL) = 4 1/2 MILES - 30 MINUTES
ST. OLAVES TO NEW CUT = 1/2 MILE - 10 MINUTES
NEW CUT TO SOMERLEYTON (THE DUKES HEAD) = 1 1/2 MILES - 15 MINUTES
SOMERLEYTON TO OULTON BROAD (WHERRY, LADY OF THE LAKE, COMMODORE
= 5 MILES - 45 MINUTES
OULTON BROAD TO BECCLES  (WAVENEY HOUSE HOTEL, SWAN HOUSE)
= 8 MILES - 1 HOUR, 15 MINUTES
BECCLES TO GELDESTON (THE LOCKS, THE WHERRY) = 2 1/2 MILES - 30 MINUTES

## GELDESTON TO BURGH CASTLE

GELDESTON (THE LOCKS, THE WHERRY) TO BECCLES  = 2 1/2 MILES - 30 MINUTES
BECCLES (WAVENEY HOUSE HOTEL, SWAN HOUSE) TO OULTON BROAD
= 8 MILES - 1 HOUR, 15 MINUTES
OULTON BROAD (WHERRY, LADY OF THE LAKE, COMMODORE) TO SOMERLEYTON
= 5 MILES - 45 MINUTES
SOMERLEYTON (THE DUKES HEAD) TO THE NEW CUT = 1 1/2 MILES - 15 MINUTES
NEW CUT TO ST. OLAVES  = 1/2 MILE - 10 MINUTES
ST. OLAVES (THE BELL) TO BURGH CASTLE = 4 1/2 MILES - 30 MINUTES

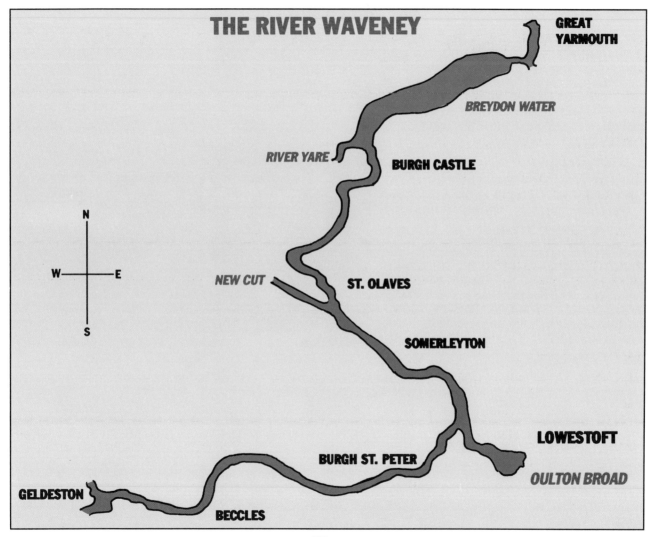

THE RIVER WAVENEY

GREAT YARMOUTH

BREYDON WATER

RIVER YARE

BURGH CASTLE

N
W   E
S

NEW CUT

ST. OLAVES

SOMERLEYTON

LOWESTOFT

BURGH ST. PETER

OULTON BROAD

GELDESTON

BECCLES

# THE RIVER WAVENEY

AT THE BEGINNING OF THIS RIVER LIE THE REMAINS OF BURGH CASTLE. IF YOU WISH TO VISIT FRITTON LAKE COUNTRYWORLD, WHERE THERE IS A CAFE, A NINE HOLE GOLF COURSE, FALCONRY, HORSE AND CART RIDES, FISHING, LAUNCH TRIPS AND HEAVY HORSE STABLES, THE ROAD FROM ST. OLAVES IS BEST.

ALMOST OPPOSITE ST. OLAVES IS THE NEW CUT, (BUILT IN 1833), AN ALTERNATIVE ROUTE TO THE RIVER YARE. FURTHER ALONG IS AN IRON SUSPENSION BRIDGE WHICH CONNECTS NORFOLK AND SUFFOLK.

ONCE PAST SOMERLEYTON BEAR LEFT FOR OULTON BROAD. AT LOWESTOFT THERE ARE TOURS TO SEE ROUND THE FISHING TRADE ON TUESDAYS, WEDNESDAYS AND THURSDAYS FROM MID JULY TO MID SEPTEMBER. GOOD BATHING, BINGO, A PAVILION, PARKS, PIERS AND PITCH AND PUTT ARE ALSO WITHIN REACH.

CRUISING ON TO BECCLES (HARBOUR PICTURED ABOVE) YOU WILL PASS THE WAVENEY RIVER CENTRE AND "THE WAVENEY INN" WHERE MOORING FEES OVERNIGHT ARE £5 (1994).

BECCLES, WHICH IS BUILT ON SEVERAL LEVELS, IS A LOVELY OLD MARKET TOWN WITH A WEALTH OF ANCIENT HOUSES, GOOD SHOPS, SEVERAL PUBS, AND AN OUTSIDE HEATED SWIMMING POOL. THE CHURCH OF ST. MICHAEL, WHERE LORD NELSON'S PARENTS WERE MARRIED IN 1749, CAN BE SEEN AT QUITE A DISTANCE FROM THE RIVER.

BECCLES BRIDGE (HEIGHT AT HIGH WATER - 6'8") SHOULD ONLY BE NAVIGATED AT LOW TIDES. ON THE WAY TO GELDESTON THERE ARE MANY AREAS FOR GOOD FISHING. AT THE TOP OF THE RIVER THE RIGHT FORK LEADS TO GELDESTON VILLAGE AND THE LEFT TO THE "LOCKS INN" WHICH CAN ONLY BE REACHED BY RIVER OR ACROSS A MARSHY TRACK.

# ST OLAVES

## THE BELL INN          TEL: (01493) 488249

**4 1/2 MILES FROM BURGH CASTLE - 30 MINUTES**
**1/2 MILE TO NEW CUT - 10 MINUTES**
**1 1/2 MILES TO SOMERLEYTON - 20 MINUTES**

**MOORINGS:**   Room for about 20 boats stern on.  There is no charge but do watch the current here and keep an eye on the ebb and flow of the river.  Distance to pub is 50/200 yards.

| | |
|---|---|
| **SUMMER:** | All day - from 08.30 a.m. |
| **WINTER:** | 11 to 3 and 7 to 11 |
| **SUNDAY:** | 12 to 3 and 7 to 10.30 |
| **BEERS:** | Different cask ales weekly, Guinness Murphys and Whitbread Best |
| **LAGERS:** | Heineken and Stella Artois |
| **CIDERS:** | Strongbow, Woodpecker and Scrumpy Jack |
| **SPECIALITIES:** | All cooked from fresh ingredients. Breakfasts. Lobster. Barbeques. |
| **SUNDAY LUNCH:** | £5.50 (1994).  £9.95 (Restaurant) |
| **BAR MEALS:** | Noon to 2.30 and 7 to 10  (Last Orders  2.30 pm and 9.30 pm) |

**DINING FACILITIES:**  Seating for 55.  Noon to 2.30 and 7 to 10 (Last Orders 2.30 pm and 9.30 pm).  Typical cost of three course meal for two with wine: £25.
**CARDS:**  Visa, Access and Diners.

*One of Broadlands oldest Inns with 15th Century oak beams, genuine brass fittings and copper canopies.  Fires are lit whenever "there's a chill in the air".  The pub has been given a face-lift and the restaurant now overlooks landscaped gardens, a pond, patio and the river beyond.*

*Background and outside music are provided and the service is quick and cheerful.  Take away food and beer are available. Children and dogs welcome.*

*The remains of 13th Century St. Olaves Priory are situated nearby and Fritton Lake Country World is a mile away from the village.*

# SOMERLEYTON

## THE DUKES HEAD　　TEL: (01502) 730281

**2 MILES FROM ST OLAVES - 20 MINUTES**
**1 1/2 MILES FROM NEW CUT - 15 MINUTES**
**5 MILES TO OULTON BROAD STAITHE - 45 MINUTES**

**MOORINGS:** Approximately 30 side on. No charge for the first 24 hours and the distance to the pub is 200 to 350 yards up the Public Footpath leading from the river. Torches required at night.

| | |
|---|---|
| **SUMMER:** | All day |
| **WINTER:** | 11 to 3 and 5.30 to 11 |
| | (All day Saturday) |
| **SUNDAY:** | 12 to 3 and 7 to 10.30 |
| **BEERS:** | Whitbread,Boddingtons, Flowers, Wethereds, Murphys and Marstons |
| **LAGERS:** | Heineken and Stella Artois |
| **CIDERS:** | Scrumpy Jack |
| **SPECIALITIES:** | Lasagne. Mixed Grill. Childrens Menu. |
| **SUNDAY LUNCH:** | Cold and main menu in Summer. Roasts and main menu in Winter. |
| **BAR MEALS:** | Noon to 2.30 and 7.30 to 10 (Last Orders 2.15 pm and 9.45 pm) |

**DINING FACILITIES:** Seating for 30. Noon to 2.30 and 7.30 to 10 (Last Orders 2.15 pm and 9.45 pm). Typical cost of three course meal for two with wine: £20.

**CARDS:** Cheque with bankers card.

*There is a comfortable lounge which boasts a piano and two dart boards. A saloon bar, childrens room and play area are provided plus swings in the large gardens which seat 80 people. Low background music and live music and jazz every three weeks in Winter. Country and Western in the Summer.*

*The moorings have been much improved and there is now a "short cut" through the extensive gardens of this pub. Dogs welcome.*

*More renovations at the Duke's Head are due in 1995 and since the owners also have the Suspension Bridge Tavern at Great Yarmouth one would hope these will be to the same standard.*

# OULTON BROAD

## WHERRY HOTEL     TEL: (01502) 573521

**5 MILES FROM SOMERLEYTON - 45 MINUTES**
**8 MILES TO BECCLES - 1 HOUR, 15 MINUTES**

**MOORINGS:** Numerous stern on. There is a charge for 24 hours which in 1994 was £6. Distance to the Hotel is 100/200 yards.

**SUMMER:**       All day
**WINTER:**        11 to 3.30 and 5.30 to 11
                  (11 to 2.30 and 6 to 11 - November until 1 March)
**SUNDAY:**       12 to 3 and 7 to 10.30

**BEERS:**         Abbot, Greene King, IPA and
                  Guest Beers
**LAGERS:**        Harp, Kronenberg, Stella Artois
**CIDERS:**        Red Rock

**SPECIALITIES:**  Seafood. Steaks. Full bar menu.

**SUNDAY LUNCH:**  Carvery. £7.99 per head (1994)

**BAR MEALS:**     Noon to 2.30 and 7 to 9.30 (Last
                  Orders 2.15 pm and 9.15 pm).

**DINING FACILITIES:** Seating for 120. Noon to 2.30 and 7 to 10.30 (Last Orders 2 pm and 10 pm). Typical cost of three course meal for two with wine: £30.
**CARDS:** Access, Visa, Diners and Amex.

*A large and imposing Hotel with glass and marble decor and a selection of bars, situated on the waterfront. Open plan seating allows for space and comfort. The large glass Conservatory, which overlooks Oulton Broad, is suitable for families.*

*A pleasant mixture of good service in a sociable and interesting setting. Background music is supplied together with various entertainment during the summer months and there is plenty of seating provided outside. Dogs are welcome.*

*Breakfast is available to river travellers and the Carvery is open seven days a week.*

# OULTON BROAD

## LADY OF THE LAKE
**TEL: (01502) 574740**

**5 MILES FROM SOMERLEYTON - 45 MINUTES
8 MILES TO BECCLES - 1 HOUR, 15 MINUTES**

**MOORINGS:** Numerous stern on. Distance to the pub is 200 yards across the river bridge by the side of the Wherry. There is a charge of £6 (1994).

| | |
|---|---|
| **SUMMER:** | All day |
| **WINTER:** | All day |
| **SUNDAY:** | 12 to 3 and 7 to 10.30 |

| | |
|---|---|
| **BEERS:** | Websters, Norwich Mild and Bitter, Ruddles County and Guinness |
| **LAGERS:** | Carlsberg, Fosters, Holsten and Budweiser |
| **CIDERS:** | Strongbow and Scrumpy Jack |

**SPECIALITIES:** Chicken and Mushroom Pie. Liver and bacon. Childrens menu.

**SUNDAY LUNCH:** £3.99 (1994)

**BAR MEALS:** Noon to 2 and 6 to 9.30 (Last Orders 2 pm and 9.30 pm)

**DINING FACILITIES:** Seating for 60. Noon to 2.30 and 6 to 9.30 (Last Orders 2.30 pm and 9.30 pm). Typical cost of three course meal for two with wine: £20. Please note that no meals are available on Friday and Saturday nights but food is provided between 7 and 8 pm on Sundays.
**CARDS:** Access, Visa, Diners and Amex.

*A happy family pub close to the water with a pleasant patio and gardens. Bar-B-Q's are held during the summer.*

*There is one large bar leading into an attractive dining area with views over the Broad. Games and background music are provided together with a separate childrens room.*

*Spot the flood level. Ask the landlord what happened in January 1953.*

*Every Thursday evening Oulton Broad hosts a power boat race which attracts a large number of visitors.*

# OULTON BROAD

## THE COMMODORE
**TEL: (01502) 565955**

**5 MILES FROM SOMERLEYTON - 45 MINUTES**
**8 MILES TO BECCLES - 1 HOUR, 15 MINUTES**

**MOORINGS:** There are 8, side on, at the pub where the charge is £3.50 per night refundable against food purchased inside. Distance to the pub is approximately 200 yards turning left up Commodore Road at the back of the Wherry.

| | |
|---|---|
| **SUMMER:** | 11 to 3 and 5.30 to 11 |
| **WINTER:** | 11 to 3 and 5.30 to 11 |
| **SUNDAY:** | 12 to 3 and 7 to 10.30 |
| **BEERS:** | Norwich Bitter, Theakstons, Directors and Websters |
| **LAGERS:** | Holsten, Fosters and Carlsberg |
| **CIDERS:** | Bulmers |
| **SPECIALITIES:** | Home made cottage pies. Vegetable Lasagne. Chilli con Carne. |
| **SUNDAY LUNCH:** | Normal menu available. |
| **BAR MEALS:** | Noon to 2 and 6.30 to 9.00 (Last Orders 2 pm and 9 pm). |

**DINING FACILITIES:** Seating for 18 and anywhere in the pub. Noon to 2 and 6 to 9 (Last Orders 2 pm and 9 pm). Typical cost of two course meal for two with wine: £17.
**CARDS:** Amex, Diners, Visa and Access.

*Over 100 years old with one large oak beamed bar and small, secluded seating areas. Children and dogs are welcome. By the time you arrive will the pile of copper have reached the £50 mark?*

*A pub in the true sense of the word. No pool table, no darts and only light background music. With its coaching lamps and pretty plates the warmth and hospitality are generated by a desire to keep this hostelry as a sociable meeting place for all.*

*Enjoy unrestricted views over Oulton Broad from the raised balcony dining area and the large tiered gardens reaching down to the patio area at the water's edge. Bar-B-Q's in the summer months.*

# BECCLES

## THE SWAN HOUSE    TEL: (01502) 713474

**8 MILES FROM OULTON BROAD - 1 HOUR, 15 MINUTES
2 1/2 MILES TO GELDESTON - 30 MINUTES**

**MOORINGS:** These are mostly stern on in the Yacht Station. The charge was £3.90 in 1994. Walk up through the village and you will find the Swan House by the side of the Church in Newmarket Street.

| | |
|---|---|
| **SUMMER:** | All day |
| **WINTER:** | All day |
| **SUNDAY:** | 12 to 3 and 7 to 10.30 |

| | |
|---|---|
| **BEERS:** | There are over sixty imported beers |
| **LAGERS:** | and lagers at reasonable prices along with standard ales from the pump |

**SPECIALITIES:**  Pate, Sole and Chicken. All home cooked food from fresh ingredients.

**SUNDAY LUNCH:**  Main menu available

**BAR MEALS:**  Noon to 2 and 7.30 to 9.30 (Last Orders 1.45 pm and 9.15 pm)

**DINING FACILITIES:**  Seating for 36. Times as above. Evening bar menu for two courses from £12. Typical cost of three course meal for two with wine: £35.
**CARDS:**  Visa and Access.

*Definitely the place for the connoisseur of good food and wine. It is advisable to book ahead during busy times.*

*A home from home with open fires, chintz settees and armchairs, round wooden tables and Chesterfields. Piles of logs lie neatly stacked and there are board games to play.*

*There is pleasant background music and live groups on Sundays and Mondays.*

*If you want to know how to make up those Cork "Notice Boards" you see in the shops take a look at the Proprietors' idea!*

# BECCLES

## WAVENEY HOUSE HOTEL    TEL: (01502) 712270

### 8 MILES FROM OULTON BROAD - 1 HOUR, 15 MINUTES
### 2 1/2 MILES TO GELDESTON - 30 MINUTES

**MOORINGS:**  Care is needed when navigating under the low bridge on the way to Geldeston. There is room for 6 boats if moored stern on.  No charge if you are using the hotel and the distance to the pub is "over the wall" if already here,  or a five minute walk from the Yacht Basin.

| | |
|---|---|
| **SUMMER:** | All day (Hotel Bar) |
| **WINTER:** | 11 to 2.30 and 7 to 11 (or as above) |
| **SUNDAY:** | 12 to 3 and 7 to 10.30 |
| **BEERS:** | Adnams, Broadside, Bombadier and Guest Beers |
| **LAGERS:** | Tennants Pilsner and Extra, Bitburger |
| **CIDERS:** | Scrumpy Jack and Dry Blackthorn |
| **SPECIALITIES:** | Roast Duckling |
| **SUNDAY LUNCH:** | £10.50 - 3 courses and coffee (1994) |
| **BAR MEALS:** | Noon to 2 and 7 to 9 (Last Orders 2 pm and 9 pm) |

**DINING FACILITIES:**  Seating for 60 in the Regency Restaurant.  7.30 to 9.15 (Last Orders 9.15 pm).  Typical cost of three course meal for two with wine: £45.
**CARDS:**  Access, Visa, Diners and Amex.

*Originally a private house built circa 1592 with additions from 1750 onwards and now listed as a Grade One building.*

*The hotel remains open throughout the year and is designed to provide every comfort and amenity. A lovely patio area fronts onto the river and food is willingly served to you there or to your boat.*

*Music is provided by background tapes. Children are allowed inside the hotel but it is requested that good manners are to the fore.  Dogs welcome.*

*Chintzy, olde worlde and comfortable this is a place to do justice to a good meal or merely entrench yourself and unwind in peace.*

# GELDESTON

## THE WHERRY  TEL: (01508) 518371

### 2 1/2 MILES FROM BECCLES - 30 MINUTES

**MOORINGS:** Steer to your right at the fork. Between six and eight side on just before the cut that goes round the old disused railway bridge. There is no charge and the pub is a two minute walk away.

| | |
|---|---|
| **SUMMER:** | 11 to 2.30 and 6 to 11 |
| **WINTER:** | 11 to 2.30 and 7 to 11 |
| **SUNDAY:** | 12 to 3 and 7 to 10.30 |

| | |
|---|---|
| **BEERS:** | Adnams, Prizewinning Ales, Guinness and Tetleys |
| **LAGERS:** | Castlemaine XXXX and Lowenbrau |
| **CIDERS:** | Strongbow and Woodpecker |

| | |
|---|---|
| **SPECIALITIES:** | Homecooked ham. Home made steak and kidney pies.. |

| | |
|---|---|
| **SUNDAY LUNCH:** | £4.50 per head (1994). Main menu. |

| | |
|---|---|
| **BAR MEALS:** | Noon to 2 and 7.15 to 9.45 (Last Orders 2 pm and 9.45 pm) |

**DINING FACILITIES:** Seating for 24. Noon to 2 and 7.15 to 9.45 (Last Orders 2 pm and 9.45 pm). Typical cost of three course meal for two with wine: £23.
**CARDS:** Cheque with bankers card.

# GELDESTON

## THE LOCKS  TEL: (01508) 518414

### 2 1/2 MILES FROM BECCLES - 30 MINUTES

**MOORINGS:** Steer to your left at the fork. Fifteen on one side which are free. A small fee is charged on the other bank where there is room for twenty five.

| | |
|---|---|
| **SUMMER:** | All day |
| **WINTER:** | Most evenings and most Sunday lunchtimes (Best to telephone) |
| **SUNDAY:** | 12 to 3 and 7 to 10.30 |

| | |
|---|---|
| **BEERS:** | Wherry, IPA, Nelsons Revenge, Norfolk Nog, Baldric, Head Cracker |
| **LAGERS:** | Fosters |
| **CIDERS:** | Scrumpy Jack and Strongbow |

| | |
|---|---|
| **SPECIALITIES:** | Hot Pot with "Baldrick" |

| | |
|---|---|
| **SUNDAY LUNCH:** | Main menu available |

| | |
|---|---|
| **BAR MEALS:** | Noon to 3 and 7.30 to 10 (Last Orders 2.30 pm and 10 pm) |

**DINING FACILITIES:** Seating for 50. Noon to 2.30 and 7.30 to 10 (Last Orders 2.30 pm and 10 pm). Typical cost of three course meal for two with wine: £23.
**CARDS:** Cheque with bankers card